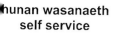
hunan wasanaeth
self service

D0504431

8.50

STILL DREAMING

STILL DREAMING

My Inside Account of the 2010 World Cup

Gary Lineker

SIMON &
SCHUSTER

London · New York · Sydney · Toronto

A CBS COMPANY

First published in Great Britain by Simon & Schuster UK Ltd, 2010
A CBS COMPANY

3 5 7 9 10 8 6 4 2

Simon & Schuster UK Ltd
1st Floor
222 Gray's Inn Road
London
WC1X 8HB

www.simonandschuster.co.uk

Simon & Schuster Australia
Sydney

PICTURE CREDITS
Getty Images: 1, 3, 5, 9, 10, 12, 14, 15, 18, 20, 21, 23, 24,
25, 27, 28, 30, 31, 32, 33, 34, 35
Mirrorpix: 2, 4, 6, 7
Colorsport: 8, 11, 13, 16, 17, 19, 22, 26, 29

A CIP catalogue for this book is
available from the British Library.

ISBN: 978-1-84737-922-1 (Hardback)
ISBN: 978-0-85720-149-2 (Trade paperback)

Typeset by M Rules
Printed in the UK by CPI Mackays, Chatham ME5 8TD

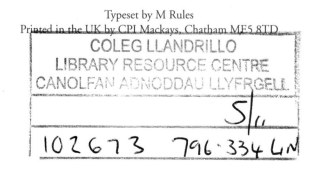

STILL DREAMING

Contents

Acknowledgements

Thanks to all at Simon & Schuster, in particular to Ian Chapman, who took me out for lunch and persuaded me that this was a good idea, and to Ian Marshall, for his diligent editing; to Clive White, for putting my words down on paper and coping with the hectic World Cup schedule; to all my colleagues at BBC Sport, producers, directors, pundits and commentators; to my agent, Jon Holmes, for his support and encouragement; to my wife, Danielle, for putting up with the constant football chatter; and finally to the British public for tuning in to the BBC coverage in their millions. Politicians please note that the British public prefer their sport on the BBC.

1

Qualifying – that was
the easy part

The great thing about England's World Cup qualifying campaign was that we qualified. The fact that we did so with plenty to spare and in some style was an unexpected bonus. Rarely have England approached a qualifying competition less optimistic about their chances than they did this 2010 World Cup and that may have worked to our advantage.

Normally the hype and expectation surrounding an England football team is out of all proportion. Never was that more obviously so than in 2002 with the much trumpeted arrival of the 'Golden Generation' – a tag for which we have the former FA chief executive Adam Crozier to thank. If it was a bit premature to describe them as such in Japan and South Korea then by the

2006 World Cup finals in Germany their time, it seemed, had been and gone.

When England subsequently failed to even qualify for the Euro 2008 finals we were all brassed off with the so-called Golden Generation, not to mention the wally with the brolly Steve McClaren, who became a handy target for our frustration. As a player, there was nothing worse than sitting on the sidelines watching a major championship without England in it. And I can tell you, it doesn't get any easier when you're a television presenter.

Someone up there seemed to be having a bit of a giggle at our expense when England were again paired with their Euro 2008 tormentors Croatia in Group 6 of the World Cup quali-fiers. Normally expectations would have been sky high because even allowing for the presence of our nemesis it looked a very winnable group. Alright, maybe not winnable, but certainly one from which we could qualify: Andorra, Kazakhstan, Belarus, Ukraine and Croatia. Surely we could at least finish runners-up among that lot!

But our spirits were still low. It was as if that sodden night at Wembley in November 2007 when our last remaining hope of qualifying for Euro 2008 was flushed down the toilet by Croatia had seeped into our very souls. Never mind that McClaren had gone as a result – water-proof but not bomb-proof – and been replaced by Fabio Capello, a man with a proven track record at the highest levels of the European club game. He was a product of Serie A just like Sven-Goran Eriksson and we didn't need reminding how unhappily that union eventually turned out.

Also, the group of players that he had to work with were more or less the same that the Swede had, only there was now a suspicion that some may have just passed their sell-by date.

Fortunately for England, Capello turned out to be exactly what the national team needed. His granite features alone spelled the one word everyone wanted the England players to understand: discipline. On and off pitch, it had declined under Eriksson to the point where he almost seemed to encourage a celebrity culture among his players. It had got out of hand in Germany with the WAGS. The team hotel in Baden-Baden was more like a holiday resort with wives and girlfriends coming in and going out and the paparazzi everywhere. When I was playing for England in the 1990 World Cup finals, as I recall, our families came out just before the semi-finals for half a day and then it was back to business for the players.

Rio Ferdinand later described it as 'a circus' but the new ringmaster was having none of it. It wasn't surprising that Capello instantly had the respect of the players. Few coaches can boast a CV that includes AC Milan, Real Madrid and Juventus, let alone one with league honours at each of those clubs and a Champions League title thrown in just for good measure. Ferdinand's comments about the previous regimes were significant. When a player of his stature comes out and says what he did it's time to take notice. He was clearly disappointed with the progress made under the previous two managers. 'This squad's in a different frame of mind to ones I've been in for a while,' he said. 'It is a very, very professional regime. This manager isn't shy of telling you what you're doing wrong. That is a big step in the right direction for the team, and that's maybe what we've needed in the past.'

What was a little surprising was the clarity with which Capello got his message across given that English wasn't his first language, or even his second or third, come to that. It certainly wasn't as good as Eriksson's. At my first meeting with him, however, I soon understood the key message he was anxious to get across to the players, which was that they should believe in themselves more. We mistakenly sometimes think of international footballers as these flash, super-confident individuals, but the truth is many of them are not. It's hard to credit, but even world-class players like Steven Gerrard can lack self-belief. You need your great players to be confident because then it spreads through the rest of the team.

Another important message he wanted them to understand was their specific tasks in the team. It seemed from early on, Capello knew exactly how he wanted England to play, which was with a high tempo and pressing high up the pitch: in other words, in a classic Premier League style. It is amazing that after all these years it has taken an Italian to get England playing like an English team should.

England were still gripped by the fear of failure at the start of their qualifying campaign, as they had been during Capello's five friendlies in charge. Looking back, it's hard to believe that the team that started so nervously in the Olympic Stadium in Barcelona against the part-timers from Andorra would eventually emerge conclusively superior to everyone in their group. So unconvincing was their 2–0 win that the general consensus among the media was that England without the injured Gerrard would do extraordinarily well to get a draw against Croatia in the Maksimir Stadium in Zagreb four days later.

As for Capello, he was positive from the start. 'My idea is to win – always,' he said. 'I don't like to play for a draw because it is impossible to prepare a game and speak with the players about a draw. It is a difficult game, yes, but it is more exciting than Andorra. I like the challenge.'

Slaven Bilic, the Croatian manager, had been in bullish mood, busily sowing seeds of doubt in the minds of the England players by saying that he didn't think England had improved since Croatia last beat them, at Wembley. Whatever England's state of health, Croatia's was rude, particularly at home where they were unbeaten in 35 matches.

'We are much better in every possible way,' said Bilic, who has never been short of confidence himself. 'We are simply better players, we are better as a team. We've had more training sessions. Before that game in Zagreb [when they beat England], we'd maybe had twenty or thirty training sessions together. Now we've had a hundred and fifty.'

However, Bilic did have the good sense to guard against complacency among his troops, reminding them that in the 1994 European Cup final the Barcelona team of Cruyff, Romario and Stoichkov had made the mistake of believing their own pre-match publicity and were duly thrashed 4–0 by a Milan team that was coached by one Fabio Capello. Little did he realise how apposite that comparison would turn out to be.

The England squad had not changed so very much since

Capello took charge. As expected, Sol Campbell no longer figured and, because of injury, nor Michael Owen, but of the younger players the only notable absentee from Capello's squads had been Manchester City's Micah Richards, who had temporarily lost his way. It was inevitable, however, that sooner or later the former captain David Beckham, who was no longer playing top-flight football, would become surplus to requirements. After Walcott's impressive appearance against Andorra most felt it would be sooner rather than later.

Nevertheless, for the game against Croatia the majority of pundits thought Beckham's greater experience and crossing ability would give him the nod ahead of Walcott's frightening pace and youthful fearlessness, particularly since Emile Heskey was likely to be preferred to Jermain Defoe up front. Also it was a game England dare not lose, so another good reason to go for old heads rather than new ones. Capello could have played both, but he made it clear beforehand that one or the other would be seated next to him on the bench. As it turned out, he opted for the company of the affable Beckham and thrust Walcott into the fray. What conversation there was between him and Beckham could only have been about the young man out on the pitch as Walcott rewarded Capello for his bravery with a performance that neither he nor the player could have imagined in their wildest dreams: the young Arsenal winger ripped Croatia apart with a hat-trick in a sensational 4–1 win. Revenge was never sweeter.

You can never be sure about young players, I've seen so many good ones come and go. Of course, the exceptional ones like

Wayne Rooney and Cristiano Ronaldo you know are going to be around for a long time, but I've seldom seen a young player take to international football with the ease with which 19-year-old Walcott did that night in Zagreb in his first serious international, having made his first competitive start against Andorra. He vowed beforehand that nerves wouldn't get the better of him and he was true to his word, turning Croatia's defenders instead into nervous wrecks with every darting run he made at them. The only downside was that most of the nation wasn't able to witness live the most inspiring England victory since Eriksson's England put five past Germany in Munich seven years earlier. That was because the ill-fated Setanta company, which had won the television rights for England games, could not come to an agreement with the terrestrial broadcasters on a highlights package. Highlights were eventually shown on Freeview's digital terrestrial service.

It wasn't just a hunch that made Capello plump for Walcott. He was well aware of how Croatian full-backs love to get forwards and having someone of Walcott's pace rather than the more static Beckham gave them something to think about. Not that Daniel Pranjic was caught in two minds: he was soon aware what his priority was, which was to stop Walcott, but the trouble was he couldn't get near the player.

Of course, it wasn't a one-man show. There were some good double acts going on at the same time, like that of Frank Lampard and Gareth Barry in central midfield and John Terry and Rio Ferdinand in central defence – McClaren's ill-advised three-man defence having been consigned to the scrapheap.

7

Also, Walcott needed the right service and in Rooney he found it. Against Andorra, the Manchester United striker had completed his fifth consecutive game without scoring, but Capello wasn't concerned. Nor Rooney. 'This was not the best of games for Rooney,' conceded the coach. 'When you start the season, the biggest players need more time to find their form. He is just married. He has to find the form. Rooney needs space to run and to work. I hope in the next game he will find the space.'

And he did. But Walcott had Croatia to thank first for unwittingly providing the service for his opening goal. Pranjic's hurried attempt at a clearance saw the ball rebound off Robert Kovac and fall obligingly for Walcott who fired it first time past Stipe Pletikosa in goal. It was recompense for not being awarded a penalty earlier when Josip Simunic hauled down Heskey. Andorra had relied heavily on the physical approach in trying to stop England, but it was disappointing to see more capable players like the Croatians resorting to the same tactic. Simunic cynically chopped down Walcott when he was through on goal and although this time he was penalised a yellow card seemed a feeble punishment. If the tactic was meant to stop Walcott permanently, it didn't work. The winger was soon back tormenting the opposition. Joe Cole was less fortunate when an elbow from Kovac stopped him dead in his tracks. It led to both players seeing red – Cole from the gash on his head and Kovac from the card brandished by Lubos Michel, the Slovakian referee.

England hardly needed the extra man advantage to press home their superiority in the second half but since they had it they thought they might as well use it. A fluent crossfield move involving Rooney, Lampard, Heskey and Rooney again ended with the United player teeing up a second goal for Walcott. Rooney then brought his barren run to an end with a side-footed finish. Mario Mandzukic pulled one back for Croatia but it was only fitting that Walcott should have the final word, courtesy of another exquisite Rooney pass.

Walcott's substitution gave the travelling fans the opportunity to show their appreciation and although his replacement by Beckham may have seemed like the changing of the guard in reverse no one seemed in any doubt about who was on their way out and who was on their way in, even if news of Beckham's 'death' proved to be slightly exaggerated. I always felt that Beckham was worth his place in the squad, if only as an impact player. He is a wonderful crosser – I would love to have had the opportunity to be on the end of some of them – and a dead-ball specialist supreme. What Walcott's arrival did mean was that England were now very well served in the wide-right position with three players of similar pace and quality in Walcott, Aaron Lennon and Shaun Wright-Phillips in addition to the more calculated qualities of Beckham and David Bentley.

By comparison, Walcott's club career had so far been something of a slow-burner. His final ball, like a lot of young wingers, was still lacking. The modest youngster hoped that this performance would ignite it. 'Before the season started, Arsene Wenger told me that he wanted me to be more aggressive on the pitch, win the ball back, get at defenders and not to show any fear,' said Walcott. When he was taken to the World Cup finals in Germany, largely for the experience – and to the disapproval of some of his team-mates such as Gerrard – it was as a central striker. Here he had found his niche. 'Virtually every match I have played right-wing for Arsenal and it is starting to come naturally to me,' he said.

After the 85 minutes the winger had spent flying, it was about keeping his feet on the ground, but Capello need not have worried. 'He has very good potential,' he said. 'Arsene is a very good manager for him. We have created a problem for Arsenal, not for me. Theo is young with a good future, but we have to help him. The national team is different. If you decide to put one of the young players in the national team it is sometimes a risk for the player, not for the manager. This time it was good.'

The 4–4–2 formation used by Capello sat happily with the England players as it usually does, but it was clear that he would remain flexible on shape. What he won't be flexible on is any looseness within the structure. He is a stickler for players keeping their position within a unit. They must always remain 'compact', as he was fond of saying. One position – or more like two – where England sometimes lacked discipline was in the central midfield pairing of Lampard and Gerrard. Many critics were convinced that the two couldn't play together. Gerrard would be recovered from his groin operation in a month's time when England received Kazakhstan. Perhaps then we would found out whether or not Capello could get them to work happily in harness. If not, unlike his predecessors, Capello would have no compunction about dropping one or the other. Of that we were sure. Team considerations always came before those of individuals with the pragmatic Italian.

The Kazakhstan players took in a sight-seeing tour of London before the game. It was a pity for them it didn't stretch north to London Colney in Hertfordshire so they could observe first-hand what Capello had in store for them – and for regular England-watchers. At least Capello was clear in his own mind where best to deploy the returning Gerrard. If a free rein for Liverpool's rampant midfielder was far too liberated a role for a disciplinarian like Capello to grant, it surely had to involve a more attacking, preferably central function. 'I know the best position for Gerrard,' said Capello confidently. 'He plays where I think it's better for him – always. He's an important player, for sure, but he's only one of the eleven.'

As it turned out, the Gerrard–Lampard alliance failed again and Walcott was less electrifying than in the highly charged atmosphere of Zagreb, not that it made much difference to the outcome. England were eventually far too strong for the team from the central Asian republic. After a dull opening goalless half, in which Rooney was uncomfortably deployed on the left spike of a 4–1–2–3 formation, England ran out 5–1 winners once Rooney switched to the middle in a 4–4–2 set-up. Even Capello had to admit: 'When he plays in the middle he is better. With Heskey he is better. Rooney is an extraordinary player.' But Capello still wasn't satisfied and he clearly didn't expect the two-goal Rooney to feel satisfied either. 'It is possible for Rooney to be better,' he added. 'He has to work every day. I spoke with him when I started. I told him technically he was very good. There are no problems with the head or feet. His movement and pace are excellent. He is an example to the other players. He runs, he comes back to win the ball. He does everything. [But] When he arrives in front of the goal, sometimes he shoots too quick. He has to be more patient. He is so young – like Walcott.'

It became a recurring theme of England's qualification programme that they performed better in the second of their double headers – such was Capello's influence – and the match away to Belarus four days later was further evidence of that. Ashley Cole, who had been senselessly vilified by England fans at Wembley, and Terry missed the trip through injury. Whatever Capello may have thought about Lampard's and Gerrard's reticence as a midfield duo he was taken aback with their humility off the field. Gerrard may not have quite concurred with Lampard's overly frank admission that their failure as a pair cost England qualification for the European Championships, but he did think he needed to be more assertive in an England shirt, more relaxed. 'I do feel tenser when I join up with England,' he said. 'I'm more relaxed at Anfield. I'm not going to say I've done it for Liverpool, but I can afford to have a one-off bad game in a way I can't for England.

'I think Fabio is a manager who's going to change personnel and change tactics and formations, both before and during games – so I don't think it's always going to be me and Frank there. But if anyone can improve this partnership and make us play together, it is Fabio and his team. As a manager, he doesn't scare me, he excites me.'

Nowadays, more than ever because of the money players earn, a manager needs some sort of aura about him in order to motivate the players – he can no longer do it by intimidation –

and I think Capello has got that. Sir Alex Ferguson has got that, so has Arsene Wenger maybe in a different way. Likewise Jose Mourinho. You have to get the players' respect and to get them to do what you want. Players will respond, if only for selfish reasons because they know if the manager knows what he's doing they have a good chance of being successful, which is what they all want. I was a pretty self-motivated individual as a player but you need to believe in what the manager is trying to do. Not all players know exactly what they are supposed to be doing. They need to be told. It sounds a bit strange but believe you me that's exactly how it is, even at international level. Some of them even need to know what they should do in certain circumstances. The great players can usually work things out for themselves.

Gerrard must have excited Capello with his performance against Belarus. He and his fellow Merseysider and good friend Rooney combined to devastating effect in destroying the opposition 3–1, scoring all three goals between them. The thought occurred to me that, against the better teams, Capello might regularly play Gerrard further forward in support of Rooney, but here Rooney was again indebted to the selfless efforts of my fellow Leicester lad Heskey. They say that a forward is judged by the goals he scores but every now and then a player comes along who proves an exception to the rule and Heskey's one of them. It was the same with Peter Beardsley whom I played alongside for many years in the England team. Without him I would never have been half as prolific. He sacrificed himself for the good of the team, just as Heskey does.

Lampard is a selfless individual, too. He is also a more

responsible player than Gerrard. As devastating as he is going forwards, he is more than happy to anchor the midfield as he did here alongside Barry. Without Ashley Cole and with Gerrard moving infield whenever possible, England did want for width down the left, as Wayne Bridge proved no replacement in that respect, nor Matthew Upson for Bridge's Chelsea colleague Terry. As usual, Capello sang everyone's praises but above all those of Gerrard. 'It is important that one player is willing to be critical about himself,' he said. 'I remember a lot of players who criticise the managers, the coaches. You need players with humility and that is important. It is about respect for other players, for managers.'

The victory in Minsk made it England's best start to a qualifying programme since 1971: four games, four wins. They didn't need reminding, though, that it's how you finish tournaments rather than how you start them that ultimately matters. I seem to remember England started rather well in their build-up to the 2002 finals, beating Germany in Germany, but it was our old enemy who reached the final long after England had packed their bags and headed for home.

Coincidentally, England's next match, a month later, was against Germany in Berlin. Capello had hinted after the Belarus game that he wanted to have a look at Gabriel Agbonlahor – another one with phenomenal pace – and his Villa team-mate Ashley Young, but it didn't meet with their club manager's approval and Martin O'Neill was withering in his criticism of international friendlies, describing them as pointless.

A good old-fashioned club versus country row seemed to be

well and truly brewing when Capello exercised his right and insisted that the fitness of Gerrard and Lampard, who had been withdrawn due to injury, be assessed by his own medical staff. In the event both were excused the trip to Berlin. One manager who might have had cause to complain was Wenger upon learning that Walcott had dislocated his right shoulder in training and would be out for three months. But the player obviously has an inherent weakness in that area of his body, having already had an operation on his left shoulder. It was a blow to both club and country and meant that England were without as many as eight senior players for the match, including the United pair, Rooney and Ferdinand. What Capello happily discovered, possibly to his surprise, was that his squad strength was more than up to scratch as England pulled off a surprise 2–1 victory, thereby inflicting upon their hosts their first defeat in the Olympic Stadium since Brazil won there 35 years earlier. So much for a 'pointless' exercise!

Perhaps it was the presence of Sir Geoff Hurst that inspired England, although they didn't need a sympathetic Russian linesman to secure victory and thank goodness it never went to penalties. The personnel may have been drastically different but England's style was still the same, which must have particularly pleased Capello – full of pace and purpose. It was a perfect example of how a successful team can make changes, even several, and still succeed and that's because confidence still courses through the dressing room. You could see it in each of the performances of Stewart Downing, Michael Carrick, Agbonlahor, Wright-Phillips and Young, all of whom put pressure on the first choice. Why, England could even afford a defensive cock-up between Terry and Scott Carson that enabled Patrick Helmes to wipe out the early lead given them by Upson's close-range stabbed finish. Characteristically, Terry soon made amends with a winning header.

If England were getting a bit carried away with their success, their next game, another friendly, brought them down to earth with a bump. Spain, for my money, are head and shoulders above every other team in the world so it was no disgrace to lose to them. However, in losing 2–0 England were completely outclassed. They contributed enormously to their downfall by being downright careless with their possession, but Spain were good. No, they were brilliant. Winning the last European Championship has given them great self-belief. This is a completely different Spain team from those in years gone by. I should know, I played against one of them when I was with Barcelona.

I remember well how I flew down to the game at the Bernabeu in Madrid with a group of my Barcelona team-mates who teased me about how they were going to punish England in this friendly. We ended up beating them 4–2 and I scored all four goals. It was an interesting flight back to Barcelona. Funnier still though was something that happened immediately after the game. Barcelona were coached by Terry Venables at the time and obviously a few of the players had picked up the odd English phrase. After the game Andoni Zubizaretta, who was both Spain's and Barcelona's goalkeeper, came into the England dressing room, walked up to me, shook my hand and said in a perfect Cockney accent: 'Fuckin' 'ell.'

England's players must have been similarly gobsmacked. In fact, England in Seville were more outplayed than Spain in Madrid. With players like David Villa, Xavi and Fernando Torres, Spain were clearly operating at a different level. Capello hinted at a lack of intelligence among the England players and one comment from him seemed particularly damning: 'Our style is good against some teams,' he said, suggesting that it didn't work against the best. 'But when you play against the South American style you have to understand what you have to do. You have to change something.' And that is the question: How much can England change? We cannot 'out-guile' teams as much as some people would like us to do. We don't have mid-fielders like Xavi and Andres Iniesta – well, we had one in Paul Scholes, but of course he's now retired. More's the pity. We have to play to our strengths. The Premier League is unquestionably the strongest in Europe. I know it contains numerous foreign players but the style of football they play is a high-tempo English style that foreign teams find difficult to cope with. When the United States beat Spain in the Confederations Cup last summer they got in Spain's faces and pressed them all over the pitch, which is what an England team can and should do. To win the ultimate prize you have to take a gamble and trust your own style of play. One thing is certain: we cannot win it playing what they call a Continental style.

A month later England returned to winning ways in beating Slovakia 4–0 in a friendly that was used to fine-tune the team for the qualifier four days later against the Ukraine. It was not a famous victory but it will live long in the memory of Beckham because it was the day he passed Bobby Moore's outfield record of 108 caps, which will have disappointed many people. I don't understand why because it's inevitable that these sort of records will be broken simply because international teams play many more matches nowadays due to the larger qualification programmes. Besides, the position of the peerless Moore in the game's history is assured no matter who passes him in caps won. I think Beckham has been a wonderful ambassador for English football for a very long time. He's been an integral part of some great moments in English football and some not-so-great moments, but he always rose above the less distinguished ones like the stylish individual he is. He could never be accused of being a prima donna, even though his lifestyle – probably more than any other player in history – lent itself to that sort of behaviour. Above all, it has been clear that he loved the game passionately. If there is one player of this generation I would love to have played with it is Beckham.

I am sure if I had equalled or overtaken Bobby Charlton's record of 49 international goals it would have been treated in much the same way. People would have bemoaned the fact that I wasn't half as good a footballer as Charlton and they would have been right. To be perfectly honest, I was just a pretty decent goalscorer. I wasn't the wonderful footballer that Charlton was or indeed Beckham is, but records are meant to be broken or, as in my case, got close to and failed miserably when on the point of drawing level! Much as it might surprise some people, missing the penalty against Brazil in a friendly prior to the 1992 European Championship that would have put me level with

Bobby did not rank as the greatest disappointment of my career – or being brought off prematurely by Graham Taylor in my final match, against Sweden. When I look back on it my greatest regret by far was losing the penalty shoot-out to Germany at Italia '90 because I thought we were that close to winning the World Cup. Individual prizes, nice though they are, are not what we play the game for.

If the Slovakia match was noteworthy for any other reason it was because it proved once and for all that Lampard and Gerrard can play together in the same team, as I had always believed they could. It had only taken six years and three managers to arrive at that conclusion. Were Eriksson and McClaren guilty of not being firm enough with each over their roles? Probably. It was obvious that both players didn't have to be used in the same way as they were for their clubs to function effectively. Here, Gerrard started on the left but roamed inside in a 4–4–1–1 system and dovetailed quite splendidly with Rooney, who bagged himself another two goals. He should be past my haul for England – and that of Charlton's – in the not too distant future and I don't expect such a hue and cry when he does!

'Rooney is one of the best players in the world,' remarked Capello, who said he reminded him of Raul 'for the movement, for the passion, for the leadership on the pitch.' I have never quite understood Raul's appeal and I personally don't place him in the same league as Rooney. For me, he never stood out in the major championships as great players ought to and it's interesting that Spain's rise to power has come after he stopped figuring as an international player.

Capello's generosity towards Rooney was understandable, though, and one little anecdote was interesting. Said Capello: 'I remember when Sir Alex Ferguson bought Rooney I saw him at a Uefa meeting in Nyon and he said: 'Fabio, I have just spent an awful lot of money on a very young player.' Now he is happy because he has spent a lot of money on a very important player. He can play first forward, second forward, left-back! I don't know about goalkeeper! I like second striker – because he's free. He runs a lot. He needs to touch the ball, to be in the centre of the team's movement.'

The Ukraine game saw the best and worst of Rooney inasmuch as his temperament remains the only flaw in his make-up. He was fortunate not to be sent off for one reckless challenge. The Ukraine posed a much more substantial test than Slovakia but the absence of Heskey or in his place a forward of real pace meant that the opposition were never stretched. There is much more to Peter Crouch than just a tall presence in the box, as he showed when volleying England ahead, but his lack of pace is a serious worry for England if they have to depend upon him from the start of matches. Andrei Shevchenko will have enjoyed his 40th goal in 86 internationals more than most, given that it came at English football's expense, but, appropriately, Terry, his former Chelsea colleague, had the final word to earn a 2–1 win that made it five wins out of five qualifiers for England and removed the Ukraine as a contender in the group.

Ten goals in two games without reply, against Kazakhstan and Andorra, during June put England practically out of sight in Group 6. The first of these games saw the return of Walcott after four months' absence but his performance was typically fitful, seemingly a lifetime away from his explosive start to this campaign, but the injury hasn't helped. On the plus side as far as the wide right is concerned, Lennon enhanced his case for inclusion in the squad that was surely South Africa-bound. Crouch may be ahead of Defoe in the strikers' pecking order but I personally like the latter who came off the bench to score a brace against Andorra. Capello is fortunate to have a player like him up his sleeve, as he must have been reminded in England's very next game, a friendly away to Holland. As against Spain, England were given a lesson in the art of possession but credit Capello for again getting England going when they're struggling – and Defoe for coming off the bench to score another brace and earn England a 2–2 draw. Capello seems to have some reservations about Defoe's size, but that's seven goals he has scored in nine games now for Capello, all but one of them after the break. Capello's substitutions are generally inspired – unlike those of Eriksson.

A 2–1 win against Slovenia at Wembley preceded England's reverse fixture with Croatia, a match that if won would seal England's qualification for the finals. How appropriate was that? And England did it in style with another thumping win, by 5–1, against Bilic's boys. Two goals from Lampard and two from Gerrard seemed apt, too. Qualification for a major finals with two games to spare? England have never had it so good! I thought we qualified pretty impressively in '86 without losing a game but our four wins and four draws didn't compare with this. It was interesting to see how in England's moment of triumph

Capello kept his distance from his euphoric players. Like a seriously good manager he remained aloof. If that had been McClaren he would have been out there on the pitch whooping it up with them. Capello knew the hardest part of the job was still to be done.

England's first competitive defeat under him a month later was not without extenuating circumstances, which had nothing to do with the fact that England were already past the winning post in terms of qualification. The dismissal of goalkeeper Robert Green early on in the 1–0 defeat to the Ukraine presented England with an uphill task that most teams in their situation would have succumbed to, but not England. They fought on as if qualification depended on it. Such spirit should serve England well in South Africa, whatever shortcomings they may possess in terms of ability.

2

Who's in, who's out and why

Begging Fulham's pardon, but it wasn't a great season for English club football in terms of European honours. For the first time in seven years, we were without representation in the last four of Europe's premier event, the Champions League – and yet the national team still managed to put the finishing touches to the most impressive World Cup qualifying campaign in their history.

In 1966, an English club was still two years away from winning the European Cup for the first time – indeed even reaching the final for the first time – and at the time of the1990 World Cup English clubs weren't competing in Europe. Instead, they were enduring the last year of their five-year ban from Europe (Liverpool were banned for a further three years, reduced to one, for their part in the Heysel Stadium tragedy of 1985). As a result, English football – it appeared – had fallen dangerously behind the rest of the world in terms of tactical development. I remember my old club Everton being thrashed 6–1 by Real Madrid in a pre-season friendly in 1987 – and they were arguably the best side in England at the time. And yet in 1990 England went on to reach the semi-finals of the World Cup, their best finish in the competition since winning it, at home, in '66, and dare I say could very easily have won it, which would have eclipsed '66 because playing at home was a massive advantage.

The club game has never been a guaranteed pointer to international success, and that is even less the case nowadays, with so many foreign players embellishing domestic leagues and providing stiff competition for the indigenous players. Inter Milan won the Champions League final last season without a single Italian in the side. Thankfully, enough English players still figure prominently in the best sides in England and while fewer may be coming through nowadays, those who do so receive the very finest education because of the standard of the Premier League. It was particularly heartening to see one such young Englishman prematurely pushing through at the start of last season and even somewhat surprising to see Fabio Capello taking an interest in him.

But there he was, the England manager basking in the sunshine at the Emirates Stadium rather than on a beach somewhere like most international managers in early August, watching 17-year-old Jack Wilshere, of Arsenal, winning back-to-back man-of-the-match awards in Emirates Cup matches against Atletico Madrid and Rangers, scoring twice against the latter. Afterwards Capello was moved to remark: 'He surprised me. Really. I saw him last year two times because he played in the Carling Cup and he has improved a lot now. He plays without fear, with confidence. And the other players passed the ball always to him. It's confidence. This is not normal, to be so young and so good.'

England have developed a tradition in recent years for taking very young players to major tournaments: at the 1998 World Cup finals they took the then 18-year-old Michael Owen, who was a sensation; Wayne Rooney was also 18 when he sparkled at Euro 2004; and in the 2006 World Cup finals Sven-Goran Eriksson, to the amazement of many, took the then 17-year-old Theo Walcott, even though he had never played a single Premier League game. Arsene Wenger, the Arsenal manager, urged caution over his latest protégé and it would seem Capello took his advice on this occasion, selecting Wilshere for the England Under-20 match against Montenegro rather than the seniors' upcoming friendly in the Netherlands, as some had speculated.

Besides, Capello's more urgent need – if not exactly a crucial one – was to find out what Owen had to offer 11 years down the line rather than what the precocious Wilshere had to offer now. Owen had moved from Newcastle United to Manchester United in the summer on a free transfer and had started positively in the pre-season friendlies in Asia, scoring four goals in four games. I have long been a great admirer of the former Liverpool forward. He is a world-class striker with something that you cannot teach players – and that is a nose for goal. He deserved to have an even longer and more successful international career, but injuries, notably to his hamstrings, have denied him this. Capello, who had selected him just once in 15 internationals, had reservations, not only about his form and fitness but whether he could contribute to the team over and above just scoring goals. If he could be satisfied on all these counts, he thought Owen would be a good player to bring off the bench in South Africa if a goal was needed.

Sir Alex Ferguson, the Manchester United manager, was optimistic that Owen could make the plane to South Africa. 'England are not endowed with a bunch of top strikers,' he said. 'The only consistent one has been [Wayne] Rooney. They've tried [Emile] Heskey and [Peter] Crouch and even included [Theo] Walcott in the World Cup squad at seventeen, which I still can't understand. There is a dearth of really top strikers in the country. That gives Michael Owen a chance. He has operated really well for us so far. He has shown some really clever stuff and I'm really pleased with him. It's only through what he does here that Fabio can really look at him. His name and reputation will not get him into the World Cup. It's what he does with us that will, hopefully, get him into the England squad for South Africa. Fabio has to pick the best players and he's not going to pick a player on his reputation from eight years ago.'

Owen himself had acknowledged that he was a different player to the one who terrorised the Argentina defence at France '98, but not necessarily an inferior one. In an interview with *FourFourTwo* magazine before the season started he was quoted as saying: 'I'm a different player to what I was ten years ago. I'm not as fast as I was when I was eighteen, but I'm better at holding the ball up, I understand the game better and I have more experience. I'm more cute and clever with how I time my runs.'

Owen had given himself the best possible chance of making the squad by moving to United where, hopefully, he would play regularly alongside Rooney, England's lynchpin. His first match at Old Trafford, a friendly against Valencia, however, did not go well and he failed to score from four gilt-edged chances. Nevertheless, Capello was impressed by his movement in the final third of the pitch and included him in a squad of more than 30 for the match in Amsterdam. However, when it came to whittling the group down to 23, Owen was omitted. 'He has not played a lot of games and he has to understand the style of United and integrate with the other players,' Capello said. 'The players need to play. Full stop. And score.'

Owen fell into the same category as his old England team-mate, David Beckham. Neither was seen any more as a major player, but, providing they could play enough games to prove themselves, both could still play a useful role as substitute in these finals. Like Owen, by moving to a big club the previous January, in his case AC Milan, Beckham had given himself a fighting chance. And also like Owen, having got to that big club the question was could the former England captain continue to get enough regular first-team football, when the loan move from LA Galaxy was repeated in January? But early season these were ones for the back burner.

Of a more pressing nature for Capello in early August was

who would he have between the posts, not just in South Africa but at the Amsterdam ArenA? David James, who had played in the manager's first 13 internationals, was widely regarded as his first-choice goalkeeper – fitness permitting, which it wasn't. James had turned 39 on 1 August, and the shoulder surgery he had had during the summer was now compounded by a knee injury. Capello must have been fearful that James's body was finally giving up. The Portsmouth keeper is a naturally fit sort of guy – he had missed only five Premier League games in five seasons – but it was obviously a concern.

On top of that, Ben Foster, whom Capello saw as the future, had played poorly in the FA Community Shield for Manchester United against Chelsea and also damaged his knee just to add injury to insult. As a result he was forced to pull out of the squad. With the veteran Edwin van der Sar sidelined for two months with a broken finger, this was supposed to be Foster's big opportunity to stake his claim for both club and country. Instead it gave West Ham's Robert Green the chance to consolidate his place in the England team by starting his third consecutive match. Capello had ruled out calling up Arsenal's Manuel Almunia, saying simply, 'Almunia, for me, is Spanish.' Joe Hart, who was on loan to Birmingham City from Manchester City, came in as cover instead and grew in stature as the season developed. The former No. 1, Paul Robinson, who had started the season impressively for Blackburn, was also in the squad. Capello said he already knew who his goalkeeper would be for South Africa, but no one was too sure who he was talking about. People assumed he meant James.

Concerns about Rio Ferdinand's fitness the previous season carried on into the new one and deepened. Capello must have been worried that, like James, his body was finally falling apart under the strain of top-flight professional football. The season didn't start well for the Manchester United captain internationally and didn't start at all for him at club level. After the Community Shield he missed the first four games of the season. But before he did, a careless back pass of the type that used to be quite common in his game led to a goal against the Netherlands. He didn't reappear for United until the Manchester derby in the third week of September. What with his fellow central defender Nemanja Vidic, outstanding the previous season, missing the first two games also, stability and continuity were not exactly the bywords of the champions' defence in the opening weeks. When fit, it's hard to think of a better centre-back pairing anywhere in Europe.

It was just as well for United – and England – that Rooney had started the season as he had finished the previous – in blistering form. By mid-September, he was already into double figures for club and country, if one included the qualifiers against Kazakhstan and Andorra in June. In fact, it was only Ferdinand among Capello's 'important' players who was giving him cause for concern: Frank Lampard, John Terry, Ashley Cole and Steven Gerrard had carried on where they left off, even if the latter had requested a DVD of his performances so far for Liverpool for him to watch while away on England duty. 'It's a DVD of his strong points and weaknesses, his qualities and faults,' said his Liverpool manager Rafael Benitez. 'He is someone who always wants to get better. It's a huge bonus for a manager.'

If mistakes like the one Ferdinand made against the Dutch – Gareth Barry made a similar one in the same match which also led to a goal – could be excused as aberrations, the performance of Glen Johnson in Amsterdam was more difficult to explain away and worryingly reminiscent of the right-back's latter days at Chelsea. The defensive side of his game will have to improve dramatically if he is to justify his inclusion in England's starting XI in South Africa. Then again, I seem to recall that Ashley Cole's positional sense was once upon a time called into question, and he managed to address the problem so perhaps there was still hope for Johnson. But in the subsequent friendly, against Slovenia on 5 September, he had another poor game that prompted Capello to leap to his defence with a fairly outrageous claim: 'Johnson is one of the best right-backs in the world,' he said. Which didn't say much for the rest of the world's right-backs.

His club manager, Benitez, must have been of similar mind to Capello because he had paid £18.5 million for the player. The Chelsea manager at the time of the transfer, Jose Mourinho, on the other hand, must have seen it as good business and would have been in the camp of Matjaz Kek, the Slovenia coach, who said: 'We had watched videos of England and I noticed that, when a player has as much emphasis on attack as Johnson, there is space behind him. We were successful in exploiting that.'

To be fair to Capello, the alternatives to the Liverpool full-back – Wes Brown, Gary Neville and Micah Richards – weren't exactly demanding his attention either due to form or fitness, so it made sense to talk up Johnson, who was one of 14 players England had used in that position since the 2002 World Cup. Not for the last time in the season, the absence of the versatile Owen Hargreaves, still recovering from a double knee operation, was much lamented.

Just when Capello was hoping to have Walcott back for the Slovenia match and the return qualifying tie with Croatia four days later – which was where the youngster memorably came in 12 months earlier – he lost him again through injury. Wenger suggested that it was the fault of the England management team for overloading his young winger in the summer. Walcott played in the qualifying victories in June against Kazakhstan and Andorra and featured in all five matches in the European Under-21 Championship in Sweden. Upon his return he suffered a back problem in a pre-season friendly in Spain.

'I didn't want him to play for the Under-21s,' Wenger said. 'I know how it works. The player comes back later than everybody else, doesn't have a decent preparation, you are under pressure to rush him back, you play him earlier than you should, he gets an injury and you see him again in October. That's why I was adamant that he does not go with the Under-21s. He has no decent preparation for the league championship, for the season and, in the end, England will pay the price as well.'

Time will tell how profound those remarks were. Across North London, Darren Bent's move to Sunderland had done nothing to simplify selection for Tottenham's strikers, not as far as Peter Crouch was concerned anyway, and he had still to start a league game, which may explain why he was left out of the friendly against Slovenia. It didn't stop Harry Redknapp, his manager, eulogising about him after he came off the bench to get Spurs back into their home game against Birmingham City. 'I love Crouchy,' said Redknapp. 'That's why I keep buying him. [Roger] Johnson at the back for Birmingham is great in the air – but how do you stop Crouch? That's why England need Crouch – because he's Plan B for England in my opinion. When the game needs changing, he can come on and do that. If you can't play through teams, you can go long to him and he gives you a different dimension.'

Instead it was Redknapp's other English striker, Jermain Defoe, who again came off the England bench to score the winner – 'Jermain Defoe, he always scores in the second half,' said Capello approvingly, and with those few words placed a question mark against Owen's proposed role as impact striker at the World Cup. Even more gallingly for Crouch, Heskey had started even though he, too, was not playing regularly for his club, which was supposed to be a first requirement in any selection of Capello's. In which case Carlton Cole had an even greater gripe, because he *was* playing regularly for West Ham. Unsurprisingly, it wasn't long before Heskey began making noises about wanting a move away from Villa Park, where he had lost his place to John Carew.

The England manager was being forced to consider alternatives to Ferdinand, but they were not particularly attractive. Joleon Lescott's £22 million transfer from Everton to Manchester City in the opening weeks of the season had gone anything but smoothly; his final match for the Merseysiders, the opening game of their season, was a horror show in which they lost 6–1 at home to Arsenal and the player was held culpable. Matthew Upson was another player under consideration. Both played against Slovenia, but neither exactly covered themselves in glory. How times change. Three or four years ago, it was a case of any two from six at centre-back. Now, with Sol Campbell, Jamie Carragher, Jonathan Woodgate and Ledley King ruled out for one reason or another, it was a case of any two from two!

One player who was being considered as cover for right-back as well as several other positions, and who was genuinely impressing Capello, was the multi-talented James Milner. However, it was the right-wing position that the Villa player coveted and that, with Walcott out of the picture, was looking like a straight fight between Aaron Lennon and Shaun Wright-Phillips. Both had started the season well for their clubs, although winning goals from Lennon against West Ham and Birmingham had seemed to give him the edge. That advantage was accentuated in the friendly against Slovenia in which both were given a half, with Lennon clearly coming out on top, his twinkle-toe feet complementing nicely those of his Spurs team-mate Defoe, who he set up for a goal. Lennon thought if he could start scoring at international level, he could make the position his own. In his 17 matches in charge, Capello had used five players in the wide-right position so it was clearly still up for grabs.

It was a little less so after Lennon's scintillating start against Croatia, which threatened to undo them in much the same fashion as Walcott had done 12 months earlier. This performance didn't have the Arsenal player's goals, but it lit the blue touch paper in the same way and led to another demolition job against England's old adversary. It may even have put him ahead of Walcott in Capello's deepest affections. 'We need a player like him,' said Capello. 'One to one, it's not easy to stop him.'

If Beckham still flirted with the notion that he might figure in Capello's starting line-up for South Africa, it probably evaporated for good the moment he came on for Lennon and the Spurs player left to a standing ovation. As wonderful a team performance as it was and as joyous occasion as qualifying always is, it tended to paper over the cracks. England could have beaten Croatia without a goalkeeper and Johnson was only ever required to do what he does best: attack. As for finding the right combination up front, that tends to become immaterial when you score five goals, never mind that four of them come from midfielders.

The other good news for England fans that month was that Hargreaves had been earmarked by Sir Alex for a return to the United team in early November. The former Bayern Munich midfielder had been out for a year with tendinitis in both knees. His American surgeon, Dr Richard Steadman, had described the injuries to his knees as among the worst he had seen in his 35 years of practice. Hargreaves' midfield holding skills have been sorely missed by both club and country, and he had not played for England since a friendly against the United States in May 2008. But there was something else to come that month that would put an even bigger smile on the face of United fans.

Owen's move to Old Trafford had not gone as he had hoped in the opening weeks of the season. He had started only one competitive fixture and scored one goal and the much-awaited Manchester derby arrived with him still on the bench. Late in the game he replaced Dimitar Berbatov and United promptly took a 3–2 lead through Darren Fletcher, only for Craig Bellamy to equalise in the last minute. Then six minutes into added-on time, with City fans screaming for the final whistle, Owen ran on to a measured pass from Ryan Giggs as he once used to from Gerrard and steered the ball past Shay Given. You want an impact substitute, Fabio? Try this for size. If nothing else, it won him a permanent place in the hearts of the Stretford End faithful. Eleven days later, having started a game for a change, against Wolfsburg in the Champions League, he was back for an extended stay in the treatment room with an aggravated groin injury. It was ever thus in the career of poor Michael Owen.

Along with Hargreaves and Walcott, the player Capello most wanted to see get back to his best after injury was Joe Cole, who had suffered cruciate ligament damage in an FA Cup tie against Southend in January 2009 that put him out for the rest of that season. He had played him against Croatia – and substituted him early in the second half – but he was still a long way from being the player who was among the very few to emerge from the last World Cup with any credit. It wasn't until late October that his new club manager, Carlo Ancelotti, selected him to start a league game – one that he also didn't finish – and it would be another month before he eventually saw out 90 minutes in a league game for Chelsea. Capello decided that the final two qualifying games, against Ukraine and Belarus, were too soon for him and set the friendly against Brazil in mid-November as a likely date for his return to the international fold.

At least Cole has had a proper international career – and hopefully will continue to have one – with over 50 caps, unlike Michael Carrick. With his ability, and playing at a top club like Manchester United, he really ought to have more than 19 caps at the age of 28. Of course, there is tons of competition in midfield, but if Barry has been able to carve a niche for himself then Carrick ought to be able to do so also, indeed challenging Barry for that holding role. He can not only tackle he can pass, two qualities that don't always go together in midfielders. And he had been scoring, too, for United. 'Things haven't worked out with England as much as I would have liked,' he admitted. 'Maybe I've not played well at the right times or things haven't fallen for me. It's not something I'm focused on.' And with that final remark he may have explained his underachievement. His display against Ukraine did nothing to advance his cause.

Ferdinand had dropped another defensive ricket against Ukraine, and his international manager and team-mates alike were finding it necessary to rally round in his defence, although no one went as far as to suggest he wasn't making mistakes. The truth was his form was just erratic because he didn't do much wrong against Belarus. Capello said: 'Rio has made some mistakes, but you can't question his value. At this moment he is making some mistakes, but that is it.'

Lampard, who of course has known Ferdinand since their days together at Upton Park, remarked: 'Rio is a very confident character. He and John [Terry] have been the most consistent central defenders in Europe over the last five years. That is the universal view. Rio would be the first one to say he made a mistake the other day. Without a doubt you need the big players and he is certainly a big player. Rio has played in two World Cups and been outstanding in both of them.'

Asked if he 'felt' for his defensive partner, Terry commented: 'I don't have to look out for him, he's a world-class player. He's suffered from a couple of injuries of late but, when he's in and around the team, he's great to have around the place. He's one of the best defenders in the world. But we're all human. We all make mistakes.'

After Liverpool had beaten United 2–0 at Anfield in late October, a match in which Fernando Torres crucially got the better of Ferdinand when it mattered most, it was Ferguson's turn to leap to his defence. The United manager accused the press of 'humiliating' him by highlighting his errors and suggesting he was about to be dropped. He had made just 23 appearances in the previous 45 games for United and England. Whatever the reason for his loss of form, be it confidence, concentration or injury – and thigh, calf, groin and back problems had all been mentioned – he did not play again for club or country for three months.

Towards the end of September, Defoe broke his hand and dislocated two fingers in the 5–0 win against Burnley. It didn't prevent him turning out as a substitute in Spurs' next match, but that (coupled with a later sending-off at Portsmouth) at least gave Crouch more of a chance to show his worth for club and country, and he started by responding with two goals in the match against Belarus, a feat he would repeat later in the season against Egypt. It also presented an opportunity for Capello to take a look at the raw skills of Gabriel Agbonlahor in a competitive match – not too competitive, though. The Villa striker could probably show a clean pair of heels to both Lennon and Walcott, and had been prolific for his club, scoring five goals in five games, but had not come on quite as much as Capello had hoped. Although he did quite well initially here, setting Crouch up for a goal, some loose possession saw him substituted and his hopes went the same way as those of his club-mate Ashley Young.

Both are regarded as ones more for the future, and at ages 23 and 24 respectively, they still have time. Unlike the 29-year-old Bobby Zamora, of Fulham, who, just as he did before the previous World Cup when Trinidad and Tobago came calling, seems to have put club before country, which is laudable. Whether or not he was in Capello's thoughts, a call to the England manager to inform him that he would need an Achilles' tendon operation at the end of the season certainly took him out of them.

Terry's problems during the season, unlike those of his England centre-back partner, were to prove more of a mental nature than a physical one, and they started on the morning of Chelsea's critical home match against United in November when he awoke to headlines about his father Ted allegedly being caught on video selling Class A drugs. Whether or not it was the previous experience of handling family problems – his mother Sue was once cautioned for allegedly shoplifting – Terry responded with typical professionalism and single-mindedness. Even though Rooney gave him plenty more to think about, he cleared his head long enough to score the only goal of the game with a trademark header to a cross from Lampard.

Less resilient was his team-mate Joe Cole, who had not performed in the Champions League away leg against Atletico Madrid and was only a substitute against United. As a result, he did not make the squad for the friendly against Brazil. He was running out of time to impress, with only one international left, against Egypt in March, before Capello named his provisional squad of 30 for the World Cup. But there were recalls for Bent, Young, Tom Huddlestone, Jermaine Jenas and Stephen Warnock in the 24-man squad for the friendly in Qatar. With eight or nine first-choice players missing, it wasn't surprising that England lost the match, albeit only 1–0, but it did raise questions about England's strength in depth. Rooney apart, the one shining success was Milner, who did not look the least out of place in such exalted company. Little wonder that he went on to be named by his peers as the PFA Young Player of Year. With James again missing out through a recurring knee injury, Foster played in goal – and he was now third in line at Old Trafford! Capello publicly expressed doubts about James's chances of being fit for South Africa, but the player himself remained 'confident'. Six days after expressing that view, the Portsmouth keeper broke down while warming up for a match at Stoke.

November had come and gone and there was still no sign of Hargreaves's anticipated comeback. It eventually came as a substitute in the last but one game of the season at Sunderland in the 89th minute. For that he had waited 113 games and 20 months, but for Capello it was enough. He would have taken him to the pre-World Cup training camp in Austria as part of the squad of 30 had Ferguson not persuaded him against it as he didn't think the player was physically ready. It was an indication of how important he was to Capello, but also how desperate the England manager was. Suddenly the criteria for selection had changed from 'must be playing' to 'must be walking'. Huddlestone was the main beneficiary.

Getting back to mid-season, at least Capello may have been cheered by news of Owen's first hat-trick for United. It came shortly before his 30th birthday in December in a Champions League tie away to Wolfsburg that consigned the German champions to the Europa Cup. It was his first treble in exactly four years. He has certainly had more joy against the Germans than I had and, of course, scored a hat-trick in the 5–1 win against them in Munich in 2001. Mind you, it was also the country where his world came crashing down in 2006 when he ruptured his knee ligaments playing for England against Sweden. It remained to be seen whether Capello shared Ferguson's view that he was still 'one of the best strikers around in terms of his positional play and his finishing'.

By the end of the year, Gerrard's form, partly due to a groin strain that restricted his training, had begun to tail off as Liverpool's season went from bad to worse. As a Merseysider and captain, he has always tended to take any failings of Liverpool more personally than most and the responsibility was clearly weighing him down. The ever-increasing reliance on another

Merseysider – Rooney – by United cannot have pleased Capello either. In January, Ferguson even declined to rest him for a home game against struggling Hull in which Ferdinand made his return. The response was typical of this thoroughly honest young man: four goals. The England manager must almost have wished Rooney could pick up a minor injury so that he could take a breather rather than risk burnout.

No sooner had Terry ridden out his latest storm about how he allegedly made financial gain out of his privileged position as captain of club and country when he sailed into another with the disclosure at the end of January that he had had an extra-marital affair with one Vanessa Perroncel, the former partner of his old club-mate Wayne Bridge and the mother of Bridge's child. This was one crisis he couldn't survive – at least not his captaincy of the national team. Capello had little option but to strip him of it and appoint the popular Ferdinand as captain in his place. As long as he was England manager, he said, Terry would never be captain again. Terry accepted the decision without complaint. As Capello would later put it: 'Terry is a leader of men without the armband.' The major fallout from the affair was that Bridge eventually declared himself unwilling to play alongside Terry and therefore unable to take part in the World Cup. It was a brave decision, but one that left England without suitable cover for Cole at left-back.

What happened next was inevitable and what invariably happens to England teams in the build-up to major finals: Cole went and broke his ankle. Ironically, the injury was suffered in a challenge from Everton's Landon Donovan, a mainstay of the United

States team that England will face in their opening match in Rustenburg on 12 June. In any other season the injury wouldn't have attracted so much publicity, but in a World Cup year everything gets magnified. However, he's a lithe, athletic individual and I had little doubt that he would recover in good time.

As with centre-back, the obvious alternatives – Leighton Baines and Warnock – were not encouraging. Milner might be a better bet and so might Barry, but Capello would be unwilling to disrupt what has become a fairly settled midfield – well, three-quarters of it. Either way, England needed to get Cole back, because he is one of our few world-class players. He is also the only natural left-footer in the England set-up, save for the winger Adam Johnson, who had come with a blindside run into the reckoning following his £7 million move from Middlesbrough to Manchester City in the January transfer window. A winger with a difference, it wasn't long before he was keeping Wright-Phillips out of the City team, which could have major implications for the England squad, if Capello is of a similar mind to fellow Italian Roberto Mancini.

When Capello became manager it is said that he identified three players who he wanted to bring back into the international arena: Paul Scholes, Carragher and King. Somewhat surprisingly, given his precarious state of health, it was the latter who was first to grant him his wish. Thanks to the judicious management of Redknapp, the Tottenham central defender was almost back to the form that made him an automatic selection a few years ago, which given Ferdinand's shaky health was a godsend. 'He needs six days between games and that's what you get at a World Cup,' said Redknapp. 'You can't train him though – if you train him his knee will blow up and it'll be no use.'

Carragher was the next to say 'yes' to a comeback after saying 'no' several times to previous overtures since his international retirement three years ago. It's just a pity that the 32-year-old isn't quite the player he once was, but then nor is Ferdinand. As for Scholes, he couldn't be tempted. Typically, Ferdinand was ruled out of the first England match in which he was set to captain the side, the friendly against Egypt, with a recurrence of the back injury from which all his troubles seem to stem. But before then he also missed the Carling Cup final against Villa. Owen must have wished he had missed it, too. Ever the man for the big occasion, Owen had scored to get United back into the game after an early penalty from Milner, but then with three minutes of the opening half remaining he slipped on the notorious Wembley surface and ruptured his hamstring. End of season. End of World Cup dream. It seemed almost inevitable that an injury, and a hamstring at that, rather than Capello would have the final say. The silver lining in the cloud over Wembley was that Rooney came on for him and won the game with his sixth consecutive headed goal.

Two weeks later England lost another from the class of '98 – and another of its greatest talents – when Beckham tore his left Achilles' tendon playing for Milan. As stated earlier, neither Beckham nor Owen would have made Capello's first XI but their contribution as substitutes could have been crucial. It must have been desperately disappointing for both players because they had done their best to get into a position where they could produce their best, playing for leading clubs. Hopefully, Beckham, at least, will make a different type of contribution from the bench, after agreeing to act as an intermediary between the players and the manager in South Africa. As for Owen, he can only look forward to the next European Championship – and keep fingers and toes crossed. On second thoughts, just keep the fingers crossed.

Even those injuries to United old boy and new could not compare to the anxiety that enveloped the nation when, in the Champions League quarter-final first leg against Bayern Munich, Rooney went down, grimacing in pain from a turned ankle, and stayed down. Memories of untimely metatarsal injuries came flooding back before he returned uncertainly to his feet, but fortunately it didn't prove too serious – too serious for England, that is. For United it was devastating. Without their talisman, they lost the 'championship decider' at home to Chelsea four days later and with him only half-fit for the return leg of the quarter-final they missed out on a possible third consecutive Champions League final to boot.

The real sting in the tail for England came from the blue half of Manchester, when in City's penultimate game of the season against Spurs Barry twisted his right ankle, damaging ligaments in the process. The recovery period was estimated to be a minimum of seven to eight weeks, which if accurate might even jeopardise the midfielder's participation in the start of next season, never mind the summer's World Cup. Barry started sleeping in an oxygen tent in a desperate attempt to recover in time. As for Capello, he just held his breath.

South Africa – World Cup winners whatever the outcome

It was not before time that the World Cup came to the African continent. Its countries had been springing major surprises at World Cups ever since Algeria stunned the mighty West Germany in the 1982 World Cup finals. African players populate all of the major European leagues and certainly European football would be poorer for their absence. It was a no-brainer that the World Cup should finally be awarded to the continent, and who better to stage Africa's first than the Rainbow Nation?

Of course, the pressure on them to deliver had been enormous. This World Cup didn't just belong to South Africa but to all of Africa, and all of Africa was going to be judged by its success or failure. It was very hard to imagine the sense of pride the continent would feel if it all went off smoothly. As for South Africa, it was reckoned that it would have an even greater impact upon life in that country, particularly the life of its black inhabitants, than the South Africa rugby World Cup of 1995, which did so much to unify the country after years of apartheid.

The sight of Nelson Mandela, the new black president of South Africa, striding onto the Ellis Park pitch, dressed in a Springboks jersey and cap, to present the white South African captain Francois Pienaar with the trophy was a watershed in the country's history and will forever be etched in the memory of South Africans like Everton's Steven Pienaar, one of the poster-boys of this World Cup.

'It was a special, spontaneous moment, and when the television camera panned round the crowd, you could see the pride, passion and sheer excitement in the eyes of so many people,' Pienaar said. 'It has given us a lot to live up to this summer, but I know the tournament will capture the public imagination in the same way. I knew that from the moment we were awarded the finals.'

The rugby World Cup happened one year after the end of apartheid, and the black people of the country, initially, were loath to support the Springboks, a symbol of the Afrikaner more than of South Africa. It was only when Mandela threw his weight behind them that his people did too. Fifteen years on, it was expected that the whole country, without reservation, would support Bafana Bafana from start to finish. One thing was certain: without the anti-apartheid struggle neither of these World Cups would have happened.

It was just a pity that the present South African football team was not as serious a contender at this World Cup as the Springboks team obviously were at theirs. As a football nation, South Africa is still in its infancy. It didn't compete in the first six World Cups and was banned from taking part until 1992 because of its government's apartheid policy. Drawn with France, Uruguay and Mexico, there was a serious danger of them becoming the first host nation not to qualify from the group stages. Their Brazilian coach Carlos Alberto Parreira admitted they had 'a mountain to climb'.

Their critics made the point that they did not figure in the top ten of those teams that even the South African public most wanted to see, but that's hardly surprising. The same wouldn't be true if a European country, say, were hosting the World Cup, because fans in those countries regularly get to watch the world's superstars. But that wasn't the case in South Africa so, of course, they were more excited about seeing the Spain of Fernando Torres and David Villa, the Brazil of Kaka and Robinho, and the England of Wayne Rooney and Steven Gerrard than their own team.

Given that, it made it all the more sense that a country like South Africa should be awarded the World Cup so that their fans could be given the opportunity to see the great players of the world in the flesh. Anyway, like any host nation that was eliminated early in the competition, you knew the local fans would just latch on to another team.

Immediately it was chosen as the venue for the 2010 World Cup, concerns naturally were voiced about security. But it was never a good enough reason not to award South Africa the World Cup. The South African government spent more than £100 million on event security, which was expected to be at an unprecedented level. Inevitably – but quite unfairly – the Togo team's tragedy at the Africa Cup of Nations in Angola, where three people were murdered by separatists, reawakened fears about security at the World Cup – never mind that the two countries were 1300 miles apart. Angolan security forces, accompanying the Togo team bus when it was attacked, were the target rather than the Togo team itself. Furthermore, the bus had deviated from the route recommended by security advisors.

It merely made the South African World Cup organisers all the more determined that their own security would not be breached. After all, the British and Irish Lions tour the previous year had gone off smoothly enough. It was somehow appropriate that Kodjovi Obilale, the Togo reserve goalkeeper, who was shot twice in the back, recovered from his ordeal at a hospital in Johannesburg.

The hope was that a nation that received so much negative press would now get the world's attention for all the right reasons, and that it would lead to increased investment in the country. It was said that for these finals alone, for every ten tourists who visited South Africa one new permanent job would be created. There is no doubt that sports like football and rugby can offer young people hope and, in the case of South Africa's deprived young people, show them that there is an alternative to a life of drugs and crime. For many, like Pienaar, football is all they have. 'For young kids like myself, you don't even dream about going places – that's the only thing you had: play in the streets, go to school and then after school play soccer again,' he said.

The fear, of course, was that the World Cup would be something that was too remote for the majority of the country and would have little impact upon its impoverished millions. Worse still, there was the concern that it would lead to the exploitation of its young people. There was no doubt that the drugs lords must have seen it as a great opportunity to make money. There were threats that the township dwellers would disrupt the World Cup with protests about their squalid living conditions – goodness knows their protests would have been valid enough, with Aids, HIV and drug dependency endemic in those areas. Hopefully, there would be huge financial and social benefits for the country. Then we would know for sure that sport really does have the power to change the world.

I was fascinated to see what the interest in the World Cup would be like in the townships. One hoped most would get a ticket, but those who couldn't, would they be crowded around television sets soaking up every minute of the action? Would they live and breathe the World Cup? These were things I was looking forward to finding out. Fans can make or break a World Cup and I was confident that the atmosphere at this one would be very special – and possibly very deafening, too, with all those vuvuzelas blaring out! It was sure to be colourful and I was expecting some great television pictures of the crowds in the stadiums.

I had been to South Africa a couple of times in the past and even had the honour of meeting Mandela once at a golf event. I knew that football was very much the black man's sport in South Africa. The South African white people love their rugby and cricket, and yes they like football, too, but this sport primarily belonged to the black people of the country and they guarded it jealously. During the apartheid era it became a symbol of hope. 'Whatever happens we'll guard football with our lives if we have to – it was our game,' said Webster Lichaba, a black African footballer, interviewed on a BBC *Inside Sport* programme prior to the finals.

'Football was vital to me. It took away whatever pain you had, whatever discomfort you had. It released you – you had so much energy, so much relief, so much joy at that time. We used to play mostly over the weekends, and that's what we looked forward to because you felt different – you were a person at that time. It was only as I got older that I started to see the segregation, even in football. In the stadiums, the whites would sit on one side of the pitch and the blacks and the Indians on the other.'

The white South African central defender Matthew Booth – who at 6ft 5in was one of the few players at this World Cup who could look Peter Crouch in the eye – learned the game playing against black children during the days of apartheid. That wasn't quite the experience Pienaar had, growing up in Westbury, a township on the outskirts of Johannesburg. 'We weren't allowed to go to the other side of the main road, because on the other side there was a lot of white people living, so when you as a young kid went into that neighbourhood you got stoned or they shot you with pellet guns,' he said.

'There were some rough areas in and around Johannesburg, but it [Westbury] had to be one of the roughest. It is hard to describe just how bad it was, because gang violence, drug dealing and shootings were everywhere. One thing that sticks in my mind is watching television sitting on the floor. We had a couch, but I wasn't allowed on it, because you never knew when a bullet was going to come flying in through the window.

'What happened in Angola was terrible, but there is a lot of struggle going on throughout Africa. People are fighting for their freedom. That is how they see it. But this is a worldwide event. The world is coming to South Africa, and there is a cry throughout the continent for the guns to be put down. For a few weeks, at least, I think people will forget their problems, forget the civil wars and have a smile on their face.'

Back round about the time I was playing World Cups, Pelé famously predicted that an African country would win the World Cup by the year 2000. Unfortunately, the anticipated rise of the African nations hadn't happened. The best that an African country had managed prior to this World Cup was the quarter-finals, which Cameroon reached at Italia '90. They were producing terrific players – Didier Drogba, Michael Essien, Samuel Eto'o – but no one country had yet produced enough of them at the same time.

If the World Cup was contested by continents rather than countries, it would be a different story, but it isn't. Countries like Ghana, Cameroon, Egypt and the Ivory Coast can each boast two or three outstanding players, but that's a long way short of the six or seven required to mount a realistic challenge. Until one country can find a greater pool of talented players, I don't see the situation changing for a while yet.

Not everyone shared my view. Abedi Pele, the three-time African Footballer of the Year, predicted that one of the six African countries contesting the event this time – Algeria, Cameroon, Ghana, Ivory Coast and Nigeria were the others – would win it. 'We definitely will have one African team that goes far and when I say goes far I mean as far as raising the trophy,' he said after the draw was made last December. 'When I make this prediction people laugh, but I believe it. This is our best chance of lifting the trophy because if you study the history of the World Cup, Brazil are the only team to win it outside their continent.'

True enough. But the anticipated mild weather conditions this time made the competition much more manageable for teams from outside the African continent, notably the thirteen from Europe, who might otherwise have struggled if the climate had been hot or humid.

South Africa, who were captained by Portsmouth's Aaron Mokoena, did well enough in the Confederations Cup last year, when they were beaten only by a late free-kick from Brazil's Dani Alves in the semi-finals and led Spain, the European champions, until the 88th minute in the third-place match before losing. However, afterwards their results took a distinct turn for the worse and they lost eight of nine games before sacking their Brazilian coach Joel Santana and bringing back Parreira, who had quit eighteen months earlier when his wife became seriously ill. Even arranging friendlies against suitable opposition had been a headache for Parreira.

It was a shame Benni McCarthy couldn't make the squad, because they had struggled to score goals in the run-up to the finals and he has been so prolific for them during his career, scoring 32 in 78 matches. However, the 32-year-old's fitness had been an issue all season at Blackburn Rovers and West Ham. He even had to suffer the indignity of being described as too fat by the Hammers' co-owner David Sullivan!

Mark Fish, the former Bolton and Charlton defender, who played in the 1998 World Cup for South Africa, had gone on record as saying that their Africa Cup of Nations victory in 1996 came too soon and it had led to stagnation; they would be better off, he thought, focusing on the 2014 and 2018 World Cups. In the circumstances, making the knockout stages would be a great success and I expected the experienced Parreira, who led Brazil to the title at USA '94, to at least get the most out of them. But if the worst happened and they were eliminated prematurely I didn't feel it would seriously affect the tournament's appeal.

Egypt, one of the strongest African nations and winners of the Africa Cup of Nations this year, had failed to qualify. In their absence, Ivory Coast, who were coached by Sven-Goran Eriksson, were reckoned to have the best chance of the African countries, but they had a habit of under-achieving. With the sort of luck that Eriksson would have been all too familiar with from his time as England coach, Drogba broke his arm during pre-World Cup training in Switzerland, putting his participation at the finals in jeopardy. That was a major blow not just to Ivory Coast, but to anyone who shared Abedi Pele's optimism. As it was, Ghana had already lost the services of Essien, Drogba's

Chelsea team-mate, with a knee injury. Even before Drogba's mishap, the Ivory Coast's chances were rated at only 28–1 by the bookies. Cameroon and Ghana were 66–1 and South Africa 80–1.

As Olympic silver medallists Nigeria went in with high hopes, but sacking the coach who had got them to the finals, just as they had done at the two previous World Cups, did not make for great continuity. Ghana, too, had some pedigree, having reached the second round in Germany and finished runners-up in the Africa Cup of Nations this year. Also, their squad included some members of the side who won the World Cup for under-20s last year. Algeria, the rank outsiders of the African six, were known to have a disciplinary problem, having finished their Africa Cup of Nations semi-final against Egypt with just eight players. At Spain '82, after beating West Germany 2–1, they were victims of a distastefully contrived result between Germany and neighbours Austria. No such danger of a similar collusion happening to them here because England don't resort to those sort of tactics and England were playing the United States in the opening game of the group.

Ivory Coast had already been unfortunate enough to be paired with Brazil and Portugal, but even without Drogba one didn't have to believe in fairy tales to imagine them upsetting either of those teams, which would have thrown the whole group into doubt. If Brazil were to lose unexpectedly, so the scenario went, it could lead to them facing Spain in the second round, which was many people's idea of the perfect final. So much for fantasy football. What we knew for real was that down

First day at the office for Fabio Capello, who was appointed England manager on a reported salary of £6 million a year. Here he compares notes with Stuart Pearce.

Theo Walcott celebrates scoring his hat-trick away in Croatia in the World Cup qualifier of September 2008. Despite this performance, he did not make it into the England squad in South Africa.

Steven Gerrard heads home to help England to an emphatic 5–1 win over Croatia to confirm England's best-ever qualification.

John Terry arrives in Dubai after he had been sacked as England captain, following a series of indiscretions.

Joe Cole celebrates after his cross forced an own goal against Japan. His arrival in the second half seemed to spark England into life and offered a way forward.

The England squad receives a warm welcome on arriving at their Rustenburg base.

Rio Ferdinand looks on dejectedly after a training ground injury to his knee ruled him out of the tournament. It was a crucial loss, albeit not that surprising.

Steven Gerrard bursts through onto Emile Heskey's pass to score a fourth minute goal against the USA to get England's World Cup campaign off to the best possible start.

James Milner is substituted after only half an hour against the USA, clearly not having recovered from a bug. Ledley King also came off at half time, having picked up an injury.

Robert Green despairs after letting through a soft shot from Clint Dempsey. For once the Jabulani ball could not be blamed.

No way through for Wayne Rooney, who was to endure a disappointing tournament, rarely finding the form that won him the title of Footballer of the Year during the previous season.

Emile Heskey, through on goal, fails to take his chance to put it past Tim Howard. Capello believed his support play could help unlock defences for Rooney.

Princes Harry and William join the crowd, expecting to see a game to make the country proud. They didn't get it.

David James was called up to replace Robert Green for the second group match against Algeria, and his confident presence seemed to enhance England's defence.

Gareth Barry was also called up, replacing James Milner, as he was finally declared fit after the injury he'd suffered at the end of the season. The Algerians were in no mood to give him an easy ride.

Anther Yahia says it all for Algeria: thumbs up – no problems here for us.

Wayne Rooney gives vent to his frustration to the cameras after a lacklustre performance that resulted in England being booed off by some of their fans.

the years African countries had sprung major surprises at World Cups and probably would do so again at this one.

Who could ever forget Cameroon's victory against the world champions Argentina in the opening match of Italia '90? I have to admit I thought at the time it was a one-off. Then when they defeated Romania in their next group match, I realised they were a side to be taken seriously. Victory against Colombia in the second round seemed to confirm that, putting an African country into the quarter-finals of a World Cup for the first time. Before England met them in the quarter-finals, we had a team talk with the manager Bobby Robson, who – bless him – said: 'I shouldn't really be telling you this but one of my scouts [a well-known English league manager who shall remain nameless] told me, 'You've got a bye in the quarter-finals'.'

Far from having a bye, it was more a case of 'bye bye England' when, with nine minutes remaining, Cameroon led 2–1. They played some of the most breathtaking football I've ever played against – and they were without about four first-choice players at the time! They were terrific going forwards – players like Roger Milla, Omam Biyik and one or two others in midfield. Okay, they weren't the best in the world defensively, but as an attacking force they were lethal. They remain the best African team I've seen, and had they beaten us I believe they would have caused West Germany problems in the semi-finals.

I wasn't convinced the new Cameroon were as indomitable, even if in Eto'o they possessed one of the world's great goalscorers and a worthy successor to Milla. But, like Abedi Pele forecast, one of the African countries was sure to go far. Which one no one was too sure, but what was more important was that South Africa ended up as winners however their team might fare. Pienaar hoped for even more than that. 'Mandela said that sport is a powerful activity,' he said. 'In South Africa it brought a whole nation together – black, white. I think with the World Cup being held in South Africa it will be even better to bring the whole continent together.'

Rooney's time is at hand

It's always dangerous to put too much trust and hope in one player – the history of metatarsals has taught us that. It is, after all, a team game. But there was no getting away from the fact that if England had lost Wayne Rooney through injury in the build-up to this World Cup, the players might just as well have stayed at home and watched it on the telly. He embodied our hopes like no other player before going into a major championship and we knew that whatever happened in South Africa, he had the potential to become England's greatest player ever. But, of course, to relieve Sir Bobby Charlton of that mantle he had first to win a World Cup.

Just a year ago I wouldn't have been quite so sure of that. But in the past season Rooney has come of age if still far, hopefully, from his peak. The departure of the iconic Cristiano Ronaldo to Real Madrid, although bitterly regretted by most Manchester United fans – and even a few neutral fans if they were honest – has forced him to grow up. Added responsibility has resulted in greater maturity, certainly as a player, and, I think, also as a person, although probably Kai, his baby boy who was born last November, had something to do with that.

Rooney always felt that he should score more goals, but with the prolific Ronaldo around it probably didn't seem quite so essential to United's success. Suddenly it was. Pushed up front on his own, he responded superbly, even scoring goals of a poacher-type nature. His goalscoring started in June in the World Cup qualifiers and didn't stop until he injured his ankle in the first leg of the Champions League quarter-final against Bayern Munich at the end of March. So important did he become to United's season, one could argue that the injury cost them the Premier League title and quite possibly the Champions League crown, too. Sadly, it was the end of his goalscoring, but he still finished the season with a remarkable tally of 43 – six more than even Chelsea's Didier Drogba, who won the Golden Boot as the Premier League's top scorer.

His ratio of league goals to games for United – and remember he has only just been converted into a first striker – compares very favourably with that of the legendary Denis Law, who scored a goal every 1.8 games to Rooney's 1.9. No wonder the great Scot has predicted that Rooney will break all his goalscoring records. He's too modest to say so, but he must surely also have his eye on Sir Bobby's goalscoring record for England. Before the World Cup started he had 25 goals. He just needs another 25 to break the record (and, needless to say, also overtake my own haul of 48), which, barring injury, he must surely do since he's only 24. I'm certain Sir Bobby would be as delighted for him as I would if he could do it. He clearly looks up to Sir Bobby. 'He's always around the club, comes to all the games and gives me advice, which I'm grateful for,' said Rooney. 'I've seen some of his goals. When the ball is rolling, I don't think I have seen a harder shot than his.'

The great novelty of Rooney's goalscoring season has been the number of headed goals he has got. That's not because he's suddenly become a greater header of the ball or, as he joked, because his hairline is receding and the ball is coming off a nice smooth pate, but because his movement has improved. It's a misnomer that you have to be a great header of the ball to score lots of headed goals. I should know, I've scored more headed goals for England than any other player! You do it just by getting in front of defenders. Look at Michael Owen, he's smaller than me, but he's scored plenty of headers. Rooney has added that to his repertoire, whereas before last season you would have said that that was one area of his game where Ronaldo – who is brilliant in the air – had it over him.

'The manager [Sir Alex Ferguson] said to me in pre-season that I needed to score more headers and since then I worked even harder,' said Rooney. 'My movement and timing have got better. I was dropping deep and probably trying to play players in more rather than getting in the box. Now I am getting in the box and it is easier to score. Since we lost Ronaldo and Carlos Tevez it is something I have had to do more.'

But there is so much more to Rooney than just goalscoring. He's got great touch, great technique, great vision, great awareness and a wonderful gift for finding space, both inside and outside the box. He's got the lot. As for the question mark over his temperament, I would suggest that's getting smaller all the time – even if he did lose his rag in England's final warm-up game against local side Platinum Stars – which is good news because I think he's a born leader. So does Capello.

'He is ready to be a captain,' said Capello. 'When you choose who is to be captain you look at who is a leader in the dressing room or who is a leader on the pitch. I remember the best players in the world – Pelé, Cruyff, Beckenbauer, Platini – were captains, no? They scored goals, too. So why not? Maradona is another example. Rooney is always a leader on the pitch. In the dressing room he's still young. Less there. But he can be.'

Before the World Cup began, there were concerns about whether Rooney had fully recovered from his ankle injury and everyone was keeping fingers and toes crossed that in the summer he would rediscover his winter form rather than that of spring. I was less concerned with that than with how England would deploy him. When Capello plays him as a second striker rather than as a first, he has a tendency to go chasing the ball in deep parts of the pitch, which is not where you want him. I think everyone's agreed on that. He did it in one of the pre-tournament friendlies, against Mexico, but it's usually when he gets frustrated and goes in search of the ball.

Oddly enough, a year ago there was even greater reason to use him on his own up front, because it was a case of Rooney and who else? No other forward had staked a serious claim for a place in the side. We fantasised about how potentially exciting a Rooney–Owen axis would be, particularly after the latter's move to Old Trafford, but secretly we feared for the former Liverpool player's brittle health and not least his place in Capello's affections. In the event, the torn hamstring did for him. Throughout the course of the season both the Tottenham strikers, Peter Crouch and Jermain Defoe, threw their hat into the ring with some conviction, but come the finals we were no nearer to knowing the answer. Perhaps Capello knew it all along. I suppose there were echoes there of '66 when Geoff Hurst made a late run into the side to the exclusion of Jimmy Greaves. Many forget that Greaves played in all three group games of those finals, so things can change even that late in the day.

It would have been interesting to see what Capello would have done had Owen been fit and bang in form, because he doesn't like to go into battle with two relatively small strikers. He has grown rather fond of Emile Heskey and of what the big man can bring to the party, which certainly isn't goals. I've known Emile since he was a kid at Leicester and he's a terrific professional who always does exactly what's asked of him – goalscoring apart. That's what Capello likes about him, and of course his ability to take the weight off Rooney. When Theo Walcott was left out of the final squad, allegedly because he didn't carry out Capello's orders, I thought of what Gerrard Houllier once said of Heskey: 'If I ask Emile to stay on the left because we need width, I know what I'll get – a perfect furrow along the touch-line at the end of the match.'

As foils go, I suppose he is ideal from Rooney's point of view. I had a perfect foil in Peter Beardsley, who of course was far more technically gifted than Heskey and did score goals. He was massively important to my career and we blended perfectly. I was a box player and he was someone who did most of his best work outside the box. It left the area free for me – you don't want your team-mates getting in the way in there! Terribly selfish, I know, but that's how strikers are. When Beardsley was playing, my goalscoring ratio was very close to a goal a game for England.

Heskey is like a big heavyweight boxer who just grinds his opponents down. He's very good in the air, which also helps Rooney, but over the years I've found him frustrating. I just feel we've never seen the best of him, that there is more that could be dragged out of him. I suppose it just comes down to the fact that he seems to lack a bit of self-belief, which I'm sure Capello can help him with. My fear is that in the big games he won't deliver, be it goals or anything else.

If England must play with a big man up front, I would prefer that it was Peter Crouch, who offers much more of a goalscoring threat than Heskey and has had a fine season for club and country. Being awarded the No. 9 jersey before the finals began seemed to suggest he had replaced Heskey in the manager's thinking. He is one of those rare players who is as prolific at international level as he is at club level. Also, unlike many big men, he is good on the deck. In fact, I would argue that he is better on the deck than he is in the air – at 6ft 7in it's only natural that he should be a handful in that department, too. He ought to be pleased to hear that. I remember a contemporary of mine, Niall Quinn, was always chuffed when people complimented him on his footwork rather than his aerial prowess. Tall players, understandably, hate to be thought of as just big lumps.

The danger of playing Crouch is that his team-mates will think of him as 'a big lump' and start lumping the ball up to him. At international level that's a mistake. Okay, it's a very useful option, as we were reminded when his header against Manchester City in the penultimate game of the season won Tottenham a place in next season's Champions League, but it's not going to work against the best defenders in the world; and, worse still, we become very predictable playing that way. Besides, England have now learned that they are better off using a crafted build-up. Crouch's critics doubt whether he can score against the best teams, but to be fair he hasn't had too many opportunities to do so. The fact is, unlike Heskey, he has proved he can score against weaker teams, and at World Cup finals you will also play against weaker teams.

If, however, Capello feels the situation calls for little rather than large, then Crouch's Spurs team-mate Jermain Defoe, who is similarly prolific at this level, is a ready-made alternative. For Spurs, Defoe has been the more regular choice of the two, but they came together with resounding success when it mattered most in that game at Manchester City. Defoe's electric sharp and can score goals out of nothing. Most of his goals used to come from a distance, but his movement in the box has definitely improved this season. He now gambles on attacking the space, whereas he used to watch the ball like defenders do and react to it; he's now second-guessing where it's going to go, like all great strikers do. I know that Ian Wright, who was similarly electrifying, has been advising him and he is obviously keen to learn.

It was inevitable that Darren Bent would be omitted from the final 23 once he failed to make an impact in that last friendly before the World Cup against Japan. I feel sorry for him because he had been incredibly prolific during the season; scoring 25 goals for a side in the bottom half of the table was a great achievement – Heskey managed just six. It was even better than either of the Spurs players could manage. But goalscoring is all about taking your chances and when tried out at international level he didn't take them. Somehow you've just got to make it happen, like Steve Bull did prior to Italia '90. He played his football at a lower level with Wolves but forced his way into the squad with goals in two pre-tournament friendlies. Bent was unlucky, and that comes into it, too, like being auditioned in what was essentially an England reserve team against the full might of Brazil.

Like most of the seven who were left out of the final squad, he probably expected it. They usually do, but it doesn't make it any easier for all concerned. My memory of those D-Days is of not knowing what to say to those who have been left out. You say your goodbyes and they wish you well, but you know they're absolutely choked. Walcott is one of those who won't have expected it. Wind back 21 months to that night in Zagreb when his hat-trick gave this England campaign lift-off and you would have said he was a racing certainty to make the team, never mind the squad. The fact is he has gone backwards since then, which I'm sure has a lot to do with the injuries he has suffered. He's been very unfortunate with them. Chris Waddle caused a furore during the season when he said Walcott doesn't have a football brain, but I would point out that he's not too dissimilar to where Aaron Lennon was with his game a few years ago, when his final ball was enough to make you tear your hair out. Part of the problem has been his decision-making, which may have something to do with the speed he runs at. Lennon has improved in that respect and so, too, can Walcott. After all, he's only 21.

Both Lennon and Walcott are 'pinch-hit' players who can come off the bench to make a difference. Lennon showed against Japan that that 0–25mph acceleration that excited so many of us in Germany four years ago was still there under the bonnet, despite a niggling groin injury. Shaun Wright-Phillips, who was preferred to Walcott, doesn't have quite as much pace as the Arsenal player, but offers more of an all-round package and gives you greater consistency. He also gives you more defensively. The main reason, I think though, why Capello went with Wright-Phillips in preference to Walcott was because of the slight injury concern over Lennon, and in the circumstances felt he couldn't trust the Arsenal player. Capello also preferred Wright-Phillips to his club-mate Adam Johnson, who kept Wright-Phillips out of the City team towards the end of the season and is a player with a bit of difference. Again when offered the choice, Capello opted for experience rather than youth, which may explain why the squad was the oldest of all the squads that were going to this World Cup. But Johnson's time will come. I'd love to hear

Roberto Mancini, the City manager, and his fellow Italian discuss his and Wright-Phillips's relative merits.

Unquestionably, the biggest blow going into the finals was the withdrawal of Rio Ferdinand, England's new captain in succession to John Terry. Looking back, no one should have been too surprised, but when the injury happened it was a devastating blow, nonetheless. It was ever thus with England teams going into major tournaments. We seem to be cursed. Better that, I suppose, than breaking down during a tournament, like Bryan Robson, my old captain, did in Mexico in '86. But it would have been nice to get two or three games out of him.

At least this way they were able to replace him – with Spurs' Michael Dawson – which they wouldn't have been able to do had he got injured once the tournament got under way, and with the squad's state of health that was essential. In these sort of situations, one person's misfortune is another person's gain; and just like Robson's injury in '86 was good news for Peter Reid, so this will be for someone else – perhaps Tottenham's Ledley King or even West Ham's Matthew Upson. Ferdinand's long-standing back condition had been a worry for United and England from the start of the season, and as is often the way it led to problems in other parts of his body. Eventually, it was a knee injury that did for him in training just two days after the squad arrived at their Rustenburg base in South Africa. It was probably his last chance of achieving the ultimate glory in the game – he's won most other things – because by the time the next World Cup comes around he'll be 35.

Fit and healthy, Ferdinand is one of the best central defenders in the world. His partnership with Terry had been the corner-stone of this England team, just as his partnership with Nemanja Vidic has been the bedrock of United's. Ferdinand and Terry complemented each other so perfectly; one man's weakness was the other man's strength. The question facing Capello now was who would compensate for Terry's lack of pace? The obvious answer – providing he, too, was fit – was King. Suddenly he became the most important player in Capello's squad next to Rooney. Jamie Carragher was a useful late addition to it, but in no way could he be expected to provide pace.

King's end-of-season form had been a revelation – and a god-send. The Spurs man was held in the highest regard by both the two previous England managers, but one wondered whether Capello would ever see the best of him – indeed any of him, such has been the chronic nature of his knee problems these past four years. But Harry Redknapp – bless him – has found a way to nurse the big man through the best part of a season, playing him just once a week with minimal training. It's reminiscent of how Jack Charlton used to squeeze every ounce of greatness out of Paul McGrath in the cause of the Republic of Ireland long after his knees had all but given up the fight. Now it was up to Capello to do the same with King. It was just as well that Capello had agreed to allow King's fitness coach Nathan Gardiner to join them in South Africa; he could become the third most important person in the squad!

It's always a bitter disappointment when you lose your cap-tain. As expected, Steven Gerrard was given the armband. It's a great honour, but I've never attached too much importance to the role. I think natural leaders on the pitch are more important and England had several of those – Frank Lampard, Terry, Rooney. From my experience as England captain, the job has more to do with what happens off the pitch than on it. I didn't find it a distraction and I don't expect Gerrard to either. Compared to Terry and Ferdinand, he's a fairly low-key character in terms of personality and he will lead by example.

With Wayne Bridge declaring himself unavailable, Capello had to choose between Leighton Baines and Stephen Warnock as cover for Ashley Cole. He could have tossed a coin. Perhaps he did. With all due respect to Warnock, we had better hope Cole doesn't get injured, too, not so much because of Warnock's lack of ability, but because the Chelsea player is one of England's key players. Full-back is one of the most important positions in international football nowadays, partly because of the space and time they get, and fortunately England are blessed with an excellent pair. Cole and Glen Johnson are such classy-looking players going forwards. The way Capello likes to play, with two holding midfield players protecting the back four, it's crucial that your full-backs are happy bombing forwards, which ours are. In the modern game, a full-back's attacking capabilities are arguably more important than his defensive ones. They are virtually wingers. Carragher isn't at all that type, but at least he will provide some cover for Johnson at right-back as well as centre-back.

I think many people were hoping that someone would emerge from somewhere to solve our goalkeeping problem, but the season ended the way it began, with the 39-year-old David

James still in pole position despite several injury problems. Capello seemed to confirm that when he handed him the No. 1 jersey upon the squad's arrival in South Africa, even though James had started just one international in the previous 12 months, the very last game, against Japan. Some people were saying that Capello should come out and name his first-choice keeper for the back four's peace of mind. But when did you ever hear a manager declaring his hand unnecessarily? In '86 and '90, Bobby Robson didn't announce who his first-choice keeper was because it was patently obvious who it was. It's just that in this case it's not obvious. Of course, it could be that Capello had already taken someone aside and told him he was his No. 1, or it could be he thought he would get more out of his keepers by keeping them on tenterhooks. Who's to say?

It's not a question of age with James. After all, Edwin van der Sar, who had just had a great season for United, is two months older than him. If he's fit, I would play James, but I do have reservations about him even then. He is given to rushes of blood, which can prove costly. He likes to get involved in a game a bit too much, rather like Bruce Grobbelaar used to do at Liverpool. But he is a naturally gifted goalkeeper. The danger comes when he's inactive; he's liable to do something crazy. He can't seem to handle that him not doing anything in a game is him doing his job. But he finished the season on a personal high with an excellent performance in the FA Cup final.

Capello clearly has a lot of confidence in Robert Green, who started in most of England's games last season, and he was the preferred choice of my old team-mate Peter Shilton; David

Seaman, on the other hand, went for James. Joe Hart is one who does look like an emerging player, but this World Cup may have come a little soon for him. It's difficult to throw in someone so young in a World Cup – and, for a keeper, 22 is young. We had still to find out if he could handle pressure and you usually only find that out after a player has had a couple of real wobblers. I've seen keepers with his talent before, but after they've committed a few howlers they never recover. He had yet to start an England game, but did well when he came on against Japan.

There have been teams in the past who have won World Cups without great keepers, but they've usually had great defenders in front of them – or unbelievably good forwards like Brazil. Or they have had ordinary keepers who have just had a great month and that can often happen. We've not got bad keepers, just ones with question marks hanging over them. It's a situation that applied to quite a few countries going into this World Cup. Spain, Brazil and Italy seemed to be happy with their keepers, but I'm not sure their confidence was shared by many other countries.

Part of the problem is that the art of goalkeeping has become much more difficult in recent times. The movement of the ball is significantly greater than when I played, or even five years ago. It's almost akin to what a balloon does when you let the air out of it. Also, players have learned how to make the ball move more. As a result, keepers don't catch the ball as often as they used to and Continental keepers, who have always tended to punch the ball a lot, even when they ought to have been able to catch it, are more comfortable with the modern demands.

People question whether the great goalkeepers of yesteryear, like Pat Jennings and Gordon Banks, would have been great today, but I've always believed that outstanding players, whatever their position, adapt.

Shilton was one of those who would have done, I'm sure. He was an absolutely brilliant keeper and one of my boyhood heroes growing up in Leicester. I ended up rooming with him for a few years when we played for England. Shilts understood the angles and over the years made countless crucial saves for club and country; but he also made very few mistakes, so few they probably stand out in people's memories – that's the trouble with playing in goal. It's such a specialised position. I mean, how many teams have won the Premier League or the old First Division without a great keeper? Not many. It may partly explain why Arsenal always fall short these days: they still haven't managed to replace Seaman.

Italia '90 was right at the end of Shilton's career, just as this World Cup probably will be for James. In fact, Shilts was 40. Some people blamed him for Germany's goal in the semi-finals, but it was just a fluke, a massive deflection off Paul Parker. My penalties against Cameroon used to get talked about a lot or, say, one of Paul Gascoigne's passes, but people forget that Shilton kept us in that game with one or two outrageous saves. That's what you need from a keeper in a World Cup: someone in inspired form who can save a game for you. They really can make the difference between being eliminated and progressing to the next round. It's such a fine dividing line.

Our midfield wasn't exactly devoid of injury worries or loss of form in the 2009–10 season, but I still regarded it as a major strength of the team. The chief worry going into the finals concerned the health of Gareth Barry. His ankle had progressed enough to convince Capello that he should go, but he wasn't proposing to play him in the opening match against the United States. I didn't much care for the alternatives if Barry was ruled out. The pundits were talking about playing Gerrard and Lampard in the holding roles, which I thought had long since been proved didn't work, not because of any incompatibility but because neither of them are natural holding players. With Tom Huddlestone left out of the final squad after failing to prove to Capello he was sufficiently mobile, the best option, I thought, was Michael Carrick. At least he knew how to play the role. King, of course, could also do it, but since he hadn't been tried in that position by Capello, I thought it unlikely. Scott Parker, comfortably West Ham's most consistent player last season, would have made a lot of squads at this World Cup, but not ours, such was its strength in his position.

The consistency and form of Lampard had been so good it made you fearful that, like Rooney, he might have left the best of him behind in the English season. England would need a few goals from him if they were to flourish in South Africa. They might also need one or two from his former West Ham teammate Joe Cole. The selection of Cole pleased me more than anything. I had been championing his cause all season, even though his recovery from cruciate ligament damage had been slow. At World Cups you need a player with a bit of magic like Cole can provide; he's the closest thing we have nowadays to

Gazza. He's a class act and was our best player, I believe, at the last World Cup. Here was an example of someone taking their chance when it was offered. He had been left out of Chelsea's starting line-up in the FA Cup final and as a result his club life seemed in a bit of turmoil, but when offered an opportunity to win a place in England's squad by Capello, he seized it with both hands. His 45-minute performance against Japan was much more like the old Cole, and for the short time he played in support of Rooney it looked an encouraging option.

Personally, I think Chelsea are a better side when he is on his game, because when both Michael Ballack and Mikel are playing their midfield is too sluggish, but I'm not sure Carlo Ancelotti shares my view. Cole's audacious little back-heeled goal against Manchester United, I still think, was arguably Chelsea's most important goal of the season. But it's hard to produce your best when your manager doesn't believe in you. Fortunately another Italian did.

Gerrard's club form last season may not have been as good as Lampard's, never mind his own usual high standard, but Liverpool's poor form probably contributed to that. At least he had carved a niche for himself in the England team on the wide left of midfield. I would just rather he carved one further up the field in support of Rooney. Even Sir Geoff Hurst was encouraging Capello to play Rooney and Gerrard together, describing them as 'arguably the best partnership in world football', conveniently ignoring the fact it was still largely unproven.

Interestingly, Sir Bobby Charlton took the opposite view and hoped that Capello would ignore the clamouring of people like

Sir Geoff and me to play Rooney on his own up front. He made a good point about how there was a difference doing that in the Premier League and doing it in a World Cup. When I was playing, people could never understand why, say, John Barnes was not as effective in international football as he was in club football. The reason, as Sir Bobby pointed out, was that in international football you were up against the very best that that country could summon, not your average Joe.

He thought it was asking too much of any player, at international level, to lead an attack on his own. But I think it all depends on the support they get from midfield – the kind of support Sir Bobby consistently gave to England strikers when he moved to a deeper role. After all, if Stephane Guivarc'h could do it successfully for France at France '98, why not Rooney for England at South Africa 2010? He just needed a bit of luck, as everyone does at a World Cup.

5

The Capello factor

Watching England beat a lively Japan team 2–1, courtesy of two second-half own goals in their final warm-up game in Graz, Austria, one was reminded of how Napoleon Bonaparte preferred lucky generals to clever ones. No one would dispute that there was an element of luck about this victory, but as far as coming from behind to win or save games is concerned, the Italian has pulled that trick off too many times during his tenure as England manager to be described as lucky. With Capello, one senses, Napoleon would have got both a lucky general and a clever one.

There are many ways in which Capello differs from Sven-Goran Eriksson, the last manager to lead England into the World Cup finals, and improving his team's performance during the course of a match with smart substitutions is certainly one of them. In fact, I can't remember Eriksson ever improving an England performance with his use of substitutes, which more often than not seemed quite bizarre.

Of course, you could criticise Capello for his selection in the first place for this match. Apart from the midfield having a slightly lopsided look about it, with Aaron Lennon deployed on the left, the team seemed to be cluttered with wing-backs. This meant that we had both Glen Johnson and Theo Walcott galloping up the right, while Ashley Cole and Lennon did likewise up the left, with not a lot going on in the middle. But in the second half Capello got England as organised and as fluent as they were disorganised and disjointed in the first half. It's always difficult to say how much a manager gleans from games like these – which are not to be taken too seriously. But I did hope that he learned that Wayne Rooney must play up top on his own – as he did very successfully in the second half, with Joe Cole flitting in and around him.

Capello didn't actually allude to any of these changes afterwards, but merely stated that the build-up in the first half was too slow and that the introduction of Steven Gerrard speeded things up, and he was absolutely right. Capello understands perfectly how an England team should play – and can play in the cooler weather of a South African winter – which is with a high tempo and pressing high up the pitch. Anyone who feared that the acquisition of a foreigner as national team manager would lead to tactics that were totally ill-suited to the English way of playing has been pleasantly surprised by Capello.

I absolutely agree with David Beckham that Capello can make the difference this time. I know it's something we say every time England embark upon a World Cup odyssey, but this time I say it more in belief than hope. A good manager is massively important. He can make the difference between a very good side and a great one. If you've got a side capable of winning a major tournament, you have to have a manager who is capable of bringing those qualities to the fore. It cannot be done with a manager who is not up to the task and that is what has happened to England at too many tournaments in the last 20 years. And Capello is a great manager, not just a good one.

He is as much a giant of the modern game as another product of the Friuli-Venezia Giulia region of Italy, Primo Carnera, was in boxing, except Capello is a giant more in the metaphorical sense than physical – and, unlike Carnera, one imagines he can fight! As Wayne Rooney remarked upon first clapping eyes on him at Arsenal's London Colney training ground: 'I think his presence when he first arrived was clear for everyone to see: he is a fearsome man, strong, passionate and wants to win.'

Although a modest 5ft 10in, he has more the appearance of a former central defender about him than the midfielder he once was. I suppose it's his craggy features and granite jaw that do that. He began his senior playing career at Roma, with whom he won the Copa Italia in 1969, which qualified them to play in the Anglo-Italian League Cup the following season. There he had his first taste of English opposition in the shape of Swindon Town, surprise winners against Arsenal in the previous season's League Cup. The West Country team, inspired by their buccaneering winger Don Rogers, lost 2–1 at the Stadio Olimpico and then ran out 4–0 winners at the County Ground, which may explain Capello's lasting respect for English wingers with a bit of pizzazz.

However, Capello, despite a persistent knee injury, went rather further in the game than Rogers. His ability to see a pass earned him the nickname Geometra and he eventually joined the all-conquering Juventus team of the 1970s, with whom he won the *Scudetto* three times, and earned a fourth one with AC Milan before retiring. He won 32 caps for Italy, scoring eight goals, the most memorable of which – understandably from his point of view – was the one that beat England 1–0 in 1973, thereby earning the Italians their first win at Wembley.

Impressive though his playing career was, it has paled beside what he has achieved as a manager. But before then he spent several years working as a television pundit for SPW – so there's still hope for me! Winning the domestic league title at every club he has managed – Milan (four times), Real Madrid (twice), Roma (once) and Juventus (twice, and twice revoked because of the match-fixing scandal) – is a quite extraordinary achievement, particularly as his old club Roma hadn't won the title in 18 years. No wonder shortly before the World Cup began Inter Milan put him top of their list to replace Jose Mourinho, only for Capello to confirm that he would be remaining with England until beyond 2012, as he had verbally agreed to do with Lord Triesman before the latter resigned as chairman of the Football Association.

The highlight – or 'masterpiece', as he calls it – of his managerial career so far has been Milan's unforgettable 4–0 defeat of

Johan Cruyff's Barcelona in the 1994 Champions League final, but it doesn't need saying that if he were to win the World Cup with England it would surpass even that. This is his first appointment as a national team manager, which, if he were to be successful, either in this World Cup or the next European Championship, would round off his career nicely.

He succeeded Steve McClaren to become England's second foreign manager in December 2007 for a reported salary of about £6 million a year. With that kind of money he could afford to continue to indulge his passion for art; his collection is said to be worth about £10 million. Not all his teams are things of beauty, though. He is nothing if not pragmatic and is quite happy to bore his way to either a draw or a victory if the occasion demands. As a man who oozes confidence himself, it was inevitable that the first thing he noticed about England's players was that in general they lacked it, scarred as they were by several years of international underachievement. With the help of his assistant, Franco Baldini, he immediately set about correcting that. Gerrard is a prime example: I really don't think he knows how good he is, but fortunately Capello does.

As a player you have to believe in a manager and respect him so that when he tells you that you are, say, one of the best right-backs in the world – as Capello famously told Glen Johnson – you believe him. 'We told the players something new on the training ground every day,' said Capello, referring back to the early days of his reign. 'We talked to them all the time because confidence was the problem. We prepared the players as they would prepare at a club, and they are good at their clubs.'

He also told the players before the World Cup qualifiers began that they were too worried about their marks out of ten in a newspaper, which seems ironic now given Capello's ill-advised decision to get involved in a private venture whereby he would rate the players' performance on the internet. The 'Capello Index' got a low score from the FA and not surprisingly has been put on hold until after the World Cup. I would say that's been his only own goal since he has been in charge.

Discipline was the next thing he addressed. He runs a much tighter ship than many of his predecessors. He insists on a strict code of conduct and you know what? Players like it. Under Eriksson it was more lax. There was a looseness about the camp when he was in charge, which was his style. If you looked at the Swede's record, he didn't do too badly, I suppose: a couple of World Cup quarter-finals and a European Championship quarter-final is respectable, but with the generation of players we had – okay, maybe they weren't the 'Golden Generation' – we should have done a bit better. Some of his senior players operated in a fairly unhealthy comfort zone: they felt they would be picked come what may, which isn't the case now, as even England's star turn Rooney confirmed.

'He's the first England manager I have played under where you know if you don't play well there's a chance you are not going to be in the starting eleven the next game,' he said. 'He keeps all the players on their toes. We know we have to play well every game. He's definitely helped me more than any other England manager.'

Before his World Cup was dashed by injury, Beckham was

nothing like the favourite with Capello that he obviously was with Eriksson. The former England captain probably knew that from their days together at Real Madrid, where he found himself marginalised for a while by the Italian after rejecting a new contract in favour of joining Los Angeles Galaxy. But Capello is not the sort to harbour a grudge and when he thought Beckham warranted selection he picked him, and together they helped Real to their first La Liga title in four years.

'I owe a lot to Fabio Capello,' said Beckham last season. 'There are a lot of managers out there who would have been pressurised by certain people not to put me back in the [Real] squad, but he stuck to his guns. Capello is a manager who will only pick you if you're at the top of your game. He doesn't care about individuals, he cares about the team. He's a manager that wants to win, and if he feels he has to play different players to win games, he'll do that. Every day and every training session, you have to be on it. There was no easy time, and that's the attitude he's brought to England.

'He's so strict on punctuality and things like that. He wants the players to respect themselves and each other not just when they're playing, but when they're not playing. In the hotel, it's important that we respect the staff, guests and everyone. With Capello, you make sure you are always ready, whether it's ready for dinner, ready for training or ready to get on the coach. Everything's so intense. Personally, I love it.'

More recently he has relaxed his restrictions on the players' use of mobile phones outside their rooms and their eating times, but that sounds like a trade-off to me and he'll want something back from them by way of effort. He demands that his players dress properly at all times while on international duty. In a funny way it reminds me of how Graham Taylor would frown on Glenn Hoddle's habit of wearing his shirt outside his shorts, although being an Italian I would imagine Capello's idea of sartorial elegance is rather different to Graham's, more Milan than Mansfield. In fact, he insisted on being consulted on the design of England's new kit, which not surprisingly involved a Savile Row tailor – and a touchline cashmere coat of just the right weight for himself!

When England sealed qualification with their 5–1 home drubbing of Croatia last September, it was noticeable that he kept his distance from the wild celebrations of the players and neatly sidestepped any attempt to drag him into them. One can no more imagine Capello referring to Gerrard as 'Stevie G' or Rooney as 'Wazza' – as his predecessor McClaren used to do – than one could envisage Alf Ramsey giving Bobby Moore and Bobby Charlton the high-fives.

The main problem for McClaren was that he went from being national coach to national manager in one move. One moment he was playing good cop to Eriksson's bad cop – well, perhaps, not that bad – the next he was chief constable. It's a tricky transition for any man to have to make and I think he fell between two stools. It would have been a lot easier for him had he come in straight from outside the set-up. He's an excellent coach, and he's proving to be an excellent manager judging by his record with FC Twente last season. He was just a bit out of his depth at the time.

The same could be said of Taylor. Graham was an excellent club manager who had a certain way of playing that was very successful at club level. I always felt he brought out the best in the club sides he managed, but he appeared to struggle with some of the star players when he became manager of England. He immediately wanted to remove the likes of Bryan Robson, Peter Beardsley and Chris Waddle, who probably still had a bit left in them, as Bobby Robson had done with Kevin Keegan and Trevor Brooking. It was the same with McClaren when he took over: he immediately dropped Beckham and then had to eat humble pie by bringing him back. No country – apart from Brazil, perhaps – produces that many world-class players at the same time, so when you have them you have to hang on to them for as long as you can.

Taylor was also one of those unlucky generals that Napoleon hated; he had Paul Gascoigne get badly injured and then, just before Euro '92, he lost his talisman John Barnes, whom he had discovered at Watford. Left without any creative players whatsoever, he resorted to the kind of football that had brought him success at club level, but the long-ball game didn't work in the international arena where players are that much cuter. Also, the English game was going through a transitional phase at the time. As a result, England struggled and he had to endure the most ferocious criticism from the media. The poor man also got it in the neck for substituting me against Sweden at Euro '92 in my last international when we desperately needed a goal, and in the process denied me the chance to equal or surpass Bobby Charlton's record of 49 international goals.

As far as I'm concerned that's water under the bridge, and Graham and I get on perfectly well nowadays. In a strange way he did me a favour by almost making a martyr out of me. The chances are had I stayed on the pitch I wouldn't have scored and I'd have been vilified along with the rest of the team. Mind you, I was desperately disappointed at the time, not so much because I missed out on the record, but because I always fancied my chances of scoring and I thought I could have got the goal that would have kept us in it. He did it for all the right reasons. It's not as though he did it to spite me – he's far too decent a man for that. In fact, it was a brave decision but one that backfired on him.

The mutterings in the camp reached a crescendo under Taylor, whereas under Capello there has never been anything but silence. You never hear any current players or even former ones back in Italy and Spain – and Paolo di Canio allegedly even came to blows with him once – speaking ill of him and that's always, in my experience, a sure sign of someone who knows what they're doing. Likewise, you never hear mutterings in the background at Manchester United, Arsenal or Aston Villa like you do at many clubs and that's because the managers at those clubs are also deeply respected by their players. When you do hear them at clubs or international camps it's usually an indication that all's not well.

Like my old boss the late Sir Bobby Robson, Capello is not swayed by public or media opinion. He will always do what he thinks is right, irrespective of what others may think. I remember times when I went through barren periods as an England player and there would be calls in the media for Robson to drop me. He would always resist them. He was fiercely loyal to his best players but not blindly so. I'm not sure whether Capello consults his senior players as Robson occasionally did, but if he does it shouldn't be construed as a show of weakness or indecision.

At Italia '90 it was misconstrued as player power when England suddenly started using a very successful sweeper system in the second match, against the Netherlands, and I was happy to put the record straight about that when I spoke at Sir Bobby's memorial service last September. It was thought by some at the time that the senior players, such as Bryan Robson, Terry Butcher and me, had foisted the tactic upon Robson, but it was his decision and his decision alone to play three at the back. All Robson did was ask some of the older players what they thought about it as any sensible manager would.

We had three great centre-backs at the time in Butcher, Mark Wright and Des Walker, and one or two full-backs like Stuart Pearce (now of course the England Under-21 manager) who could push on, so it made sense to us to go that way, particularly against a Dutch side that was strong in midfield and possessed some great attacking players in Ruud Gullit and Marco van Basten. Bobby ummed and ahhed about it right up until the last moment and finally decided to go with the system. It was a brave decision and a successful one because it got us a well-earned draw against the Dutch and then carried us right through to the semi-finals. But if he had decided against it we still would have backed his judgement.

Capello's preferred formation throughout the qualifiers has been basically 4–4–2 with the odd tweak like Gerrard moving in from the wide left. A number of pundits, including myself, believed that Capello should play Rooney on his own up front – as he has done this very successfully for United – with close support from Gerrard or Joe Cole. I wasn't sure what the players' view on this was, or even whether they were consulted, but I knew that if Capello chose to play that way – and he had already experimented with it, in the second half of the friendly against Japan – it would be because he had come to that conclusion himself. It wouldn't be because he had bowed to media pressure – thank goodness. If the media had picked the team in 1966 we would have played with wingers, Jimmy Greaves would have started every game when he was fit – and we probably wouldn't have won the World Cup!

I just hoped that Capello, in his infinite wisdom, shared my view that that was the way to proceed, particularly against the better sides that this World Cup would inevitably throw up, although I know he liked the freedom that second striker afforded Rooney. Gerrard had complemented Fernando Torres quite beautifully in this way for Liverpool and I was dying to see him replicate that relationship with Rooney. Joe Cole had been briefly deployed in the role against Japan and, as I expected, did rather well at it.

One thing is certain: against the Spains and Brazils of this world, it was obvious England would have to put more bodies in midfield. With the way they could thread the ball through you, it would be suicide to play with two up front against them.

They would rip you apart. Rooney was more than capable of holding the ball up and bringing his midfielders into play. His versatility was key to England's success. The alternative would have been to play with a really narrow four in midfield and rely on Johnson and Ashley Cole to supply the width, which they would largely have to do anyway.

Having said that, the thing about World Cups is they're an ever-changing story and the formations and tactics that you painstakingly practised and perfected in the build-up often go out the window once the competition begins. Also, the personnel you start out with, more often than not, aren't the same as that with which you end up. Take the Mexico World Cup in '86 for example. England started with me and Mark Hateley up front, but after taking just one point from the first two games Robson changed it dramatically. Losing Bryan Robson and Ray Wilkins, through injury and suspension respectively, against Morocco he was obliged to change the midfield, bringing in Peter Reid and Steve Hodge, but he also replaced Hateley with Peter Beardsley, which meant playing two relatively small men up front. It was a huge gamble but one that paid off handsomely because Peter and I hit it off immediately and in our next match we beat Poland 3–0 with a hat-trick from yours truly.

Over the years England teams have devised numerous ways of bringing about their own downfall at major competitions, from accidentally injuring metatarsals to shooting themselves in the foot with a sending-off, but by far the most popular has been by means of the penalty shoot-out. I was greatly heartened to hear that Capello's players practised them regularly. I've never understood why teams don't. I've heard the explanation why not umpteen times down the years, which is that you cannot replicate match conditions in practice. Well, of course you can't. All I know is that it doesn't half help your confidence if, when you step up to take one, you've already banged in 40 or 50 in practice that day. The pressure is obviously greater but the technique remains the same. Yes, the old axiom about practice makes perfect even applies to penalties – if not exactly makes perfect it certainly makes a whole lot better.

It's the same with golf, if you've practised a thousand five-footers it's got to help you – and certainly better than going in blind – when it comes to sinking one in competition. The size of the ball, be it football or golf, remains the same. So does the size of the goal or the hole. The pressure is all in your head, and one way of relieving some of that pressure is to know that you've done all you can by way of preparation for that moment.

There must be something wrong with me, but I actually enjoyed the moment. I don't know if it was a touch of arrogance on my part or simply the fact that I always fancied myself to score, particularly from 12 yards. If it had been from 30 yards, forget it. Taking a penalty in a World Cup is the ultimate test of your nerve. It's a position very few people find themselves in – you might say, 'thank God'. It's terrifying, like riding a big dipper, but you've got to enjoy it. You've just got to make it happen.

Come Italia '90, I'd been playing for England for four years and we'd had just one penalty in all that time, in a match that I missed through injury. Then, with nine minutes to go, trailing

2–1 to Cameroon in the quarter-finals, I was upended in the box. As I was the designated penalty-taker, I used to think about what kind of penalty I would hit if we got one and I would just practise that penalty alone in training. Two days before the game we had an open practice session and there were lots of journalists and people milling around so I decided not to practise my penalties. Robson said to me, 'You not practising them today?' and I replied, 'No, too many people around.' So he said, 'Why don't you hit a load in the other corner?' So I did.

I remember when the referee blew for the penalty my first thought was, 'Great! We're back in it.' And then I thought, 'Oh, blimey, I've got to take it.' I also thought about my brother Wayne, who used to be so terrified about me taking penalties for England that when he watched the games at home on television he would hide behind the sofa and watch it through his fingers. As I took it, I saw the keeper diving towards the opposite post. Whether or not he'd been tipped off I'll never know, but I'm glad I practised them that day, albeit penalties that I had no intention of taking when it came to the real thing!

I can't imagine a man like Capello leaving anything to chance. Besides, I understand he rather likes penalties or at least prefers them to the recognised alternative. He tells a story of how, when playing for Roma against Gornik Zabrze in the 1970 Cup-Winners' Cup semi-finals, they drew the first leg in Rome 1–1 and the second leg in Poland 2–2. Under today's rules the Italians would have won on the away-goals rule but in those days it had to go to a third game, in Strasbourg, which also ended in a draw after extra time. The match was eventually settled by the toss of a coin. The Roma captain called heads and lost. 'So I look at penalty shoot-outs as an opportunity,' he said. 'You have a chance. The best players can still win.'

With a second-round match against Germany a distinct possibility in South Africa, I hope he's right – and this time the best team do win. Anyway, it's about time we had a lucky general.

6

The same old story

I suppose we should have been used to it by now, but Rio
Ferdinand's withdrawal from the squad during the final days of
build-up to this World Cup was a hammer blow, if he will
excuse an old West Ham cliché. It's not as though it was totally
unexpected, even if it was a new injury, but when it came it still
had a devastating effect – goodness knows how badly the players felt it. The fact that he was the captain, albeit a very new one,
seemed to make it that much worse.

As I say, it wasn't a surprise to me, because I wrote in my
Mail on Sunday column three months earlier that I wasn't
convinced he would be fit enough to lead England at the
finals. As a result, our chances of winning the competition had

diminished – he was, after all, one of our key players – although I never thought we were among the favourites anyway. That's not to say we couldn't do well in this competition.

It was still a strong group of players that Fabio Capello had at his disposal, and if Fabio could do a Harry and get four or five games – hopefully, England's last four or five out of seven – from Ledley King, I still believed we could win it. Nursing the Tottenham central defender's chronic knee condition through this tournament, as his club manager Harry Redknapp had done throughout last season, was going to be crucial to England's chances.

The country was obviously fully behind the players as it always is. I couldn't believe the backing the team got for the friendly against Mexico at Wembley before the finals, because it wasn't a great performance by England, but the fans gave them a wonderful send-off. If that didn't make them proud enough, I didn't know what would. The bunting had been in evidence for weeks, with St George flags flying outside of car windows everywhere. The rollercoaster ride had begun. There would be highs and lows, great football and bad football, moments of inspiration and moments of madness. And all the while the public's expectations of the England team would remain ridiculously high until, in all probability, it ended in tears. You just prayed that the ride would last a little longer than normal.

With regards to Ferdinand's withdrawal, I suppose things could have been worse: we could have lost one of the fitter players, like Wayne Rooney or Frank Lampard. For me, it was just one of several echoes of Italia '90. We also lost our captain,

Bryan Robson, through injury at that World Cup, although in his case during the second match, against the Netherlands – just like in Mexico four years earlier. We also had a goalkeeper in Peter Shilton who believed that life began at 40 – as David James presumably does – and we had a bit of versatility, which I think this squad also had.

People needed to remember that players often miraculously come of age at these sorts of events. I can assure you losing Robbo seemed every bit as catastrophic as losing Ferdinand must have seemed to his team-mates. But in Robbo's absence David Platt took the opportunity to make a name for himself and there was no reason why someone in this squad couldn't do the same. Another similarity between the two squads was the number of players for whom it was likely to be their last World Cup hurrah. In Italy it was Shilton, Robson, Terry Butcher, Chris Waddle, Peter Beardsley . . . Gary Lineker. Here it was James, Ferdinand, King, Steven Gerrard, Frank Lampard and John Terry.

When misfortune strikes a group, it's easy to start feeling sorry for yourself, but you have to remind yourself that other teams are going through similar trials and tribulations. Some would find it hard to credit, but Spanish friends of mine were saying that they didn't think their side could do it again so soon after their European Championship success, that their defence didn't look quite as strong as two years ago and there were doubts about whether Fernando Torres would be flying after his injury issues; France had been struggling to score goals and didn't believe their manager could bring out the best in their players; Brazil's critics were saying they didn't have the flair play-ers of old; Germany's were saying they simply didn't have the quality of old; and Italy's were just plain too old: okay, Inter Milan had won the Champions League but there wasn't a single Italian in their starting line-up. It's only human nature for play-ers to look at their team and ask, 'What's wrong with us?' but it was up to the managers of those countries to emphasise 'What's right about us'. Hopefully, that's what a wise old bird like Capello would do.

Much had been written about the folly of inviting David Beckham to be a part of the squad after his injury had forced him out of it, but whether he could make an input tactically or not – and it's unlikely Capello would have wanted him to – was not the point; he added to the team's solidarity, as did Ferdinand with his decision to stay on after his injury until after the first game. It all helped make for a better team spirit, and at World Cups that's hugely important and has always been one of England's strong suits. Capello recognised that fact immediately upon taking over as manager.

I still thought the weather was going to be a big plus in our favour. I would love to have played at a World Cup where the conditions suited us right down to the not-so-firm ground. At Mexico in 1986, my England team-mates and I had severe heat and altitude to contend with – not to mention some dodgy pitches. In Italy four years later, it was a beautifully warm summer – if you happened to be a holidaymaker. Neither coun-try's climate was conducive to the English way of playing, i.e. with a high tempo, pressing high up the pitch. But South

Africa's was. Altitude would be a factor, but not like it was in Mexico and obviously not where England would play two of their group matches, in Cape Town and Port Elizabeth. Even the altitude in Rustenburg, where they played their first match, was only half that of Mexico City.

The poor showing of English clubs in Europe – Fulham apart – was also to England's advantage. For the first time in seven years none was involved after the quarter-finals – and Chelsea didn't even get that far, which meant that the England players at those clubs came into the competition fresher than would normally be the case. Prior to Italia '90 English clubs were still banned from European competition.

It was just as well, though, that Capello had shied away from forecasting a victory, as Alf Ramsey had famously done three years before the 1966 World Cup. South Africa in winter may have felt a bit like home but it was still a foreign country, with foreign crowds and foreign pitches. All the way along, Capello had said that making the semi-finals was the minimum he expected of his team and I, too, thought they were capable of at least emulating the class of '90.

It's been said that English footballers are not good tourists, that they're not as used to the regimen of training camps as some of the European players are, not as good at relieving the boredom. That may be true, but all players are the same inasmuch as they cannot wait for the action to start – even other teams' action – because they're engrossed in the tournament then. They're not going to get homesick because they're playing in a World Cup, the biggest event of their lives. It's the ten days or so of build-up beforehand that was tedious, but, of course, nowadays, with new technology, players have much more with which to relieve their boredom. Once the games start, they'll be watching a lot of football when they're not playing it. We would gather in one room and watch it on a big telly and have little bets on the outcome – Shilton and I were invariably the bookies.

You do need some light relief from time to time, and so it's helpful if you've got one or two characters in the squad. In 1990, we had Gazza – that was enough for any squad! I've never known anyone quite like him. He was constantly messing about, getting up to all kinds of mischief, usually silly stunts, some of which are unrepeatable. Bobby Robson described him as daft as a brush and he was all of that and more. I remember once in Italy we were on our way back from training or somewhere and the bus had stopped so we could buy some ice cream. Later we pulled up at some lights and a motorcyclist drew alongside us. Gazza reached out of the window and stuck a cornet on the end of his nose. He chased us for miles. Very, very silly but very, very funny.

I remember on the day of the quarter-final against Cameroon, he went and played a tennis match in the heat of the afternoon against some German tourist who was staying at the hotel. Robson had to physically pull him off the court. Then there was the time when we were together at Tottenham and he had this camper van he'd bought for his dad. Whenever he had something new, he had to show it off and he brought this van to the club one day, just before we left for an away game, and put a road traffic cone that was lying around on the roof of it.

We had a helper at the club called John, who would do anything for the players, and he said to John, 'Do me a favour, John, will you? Someone's put that cone on the roof of my van. Will you get it off?' As soon as the guy had climbed up the ladder on the back of it to get it off, Gazza jumped in the van, started it up and roared off out of the car park with poor old John hanging on for dear life at the back. He took it up the road and then accelerated around a roundabout, by which time John was practically horizontal, hanging on at the back. It was one of the most terrifying things I've ever seen, but also one of the funniest. As he drove back into the car park, with John still screaming out loud, Terry Venables, the manager, walked out of his office, took one look at the scene and said, 'I don't really want to be seeing this, do I?' and turned round and went back to his office. Unfortunately, with Gazza, he didn't quite know where to draw the line, but then very few did.

Life as a broadcaster is fairly dull and normal by comparison – thank goodness. But attending a World Cup is still exciting, it's just a different kind of excitement. When you're a player, there's so much expectation it becomes quite intimidating. When you're in the media, you can enjoy it without the pressure to perform. If I fluffed my opening line of a World Cup semi-final nobody's going to care except myself – and perhaps my producer. But if you miss a penalty kick in the shoot-out that mistake is going to stay with you for the rest of your life. On the other hand, you don't get any glory from being the television presenter of an English triumph – in fact, I'm greatly envious of them. But I was praying for them to succeed because my ambition since I entered broadcasting had been to utter the words: 'England have won the World Cup!'

It was fantastic to be a part of the biggest television audiences you would ever get in this country. I knew that if England could make the knockout stages, interest would grow and grow and we'd be broadcasting to pretty much the whole nation – and that's exciting in itself. It would be the one time you would hear me putting in my penny's worth because I do get emotional about these things – I'm just like any other fan at home. I badly want us to win and when things go awry my frustrations are there for all to see.

And just like any ordinary fan, my knowledge of the other teams and players would grow and grow throughout the tournament. I already knew most of the European players from covering the Champions League. In addition, before the finals the BBC had issued us with something they called the World Cup Bible – it's the thickest book you've ever seen – which contained all the biographical details about every team and player anyone could ever want for. As well as that, every day we would receive reams and reams of statistics which I would pore over, looking for obscure facts and figures that I thought would interest or amuse the viewers. Personally, I liked the random, nonsensical ones that nobody could possibly care about.

Hopefully, it would all make for a more enjoyable World Cup. Whether playing in them or watching them, I just love World Cups. It was one of the reasons why I took the stance I did over the Lord Triesman tapes. I desperately want England to stage the 2018 World Cup and when I was invited to become an ambassador for the bid, I could not have been more honoured. Then, in May of this year, the newspaper I wrote a column for – the *Mail on Sunday* – ran a story in which Lord Triesman, the chairman of the Football Association and of its 2018 bid committee, claimed that there was 'some evidence' that Spain were prepared to withdraw their bid to stage the 2018 World Cup if Russia, who also want to host the event, helped them bribe referees at this year's World Cup. The claims came in a secretly taped conversation that he had with a former female government aide.

I have worked for newspapers who have run these kind of entrapment stories before, and while I have no objection to those which expose corruption or some other criminal activity, I felt this one crossed the line between fair game and foul play. When news of the story was brought to my attention before publication, I asked if I could write a column on the subject, which obviously would have been heavily critical of the newspaper. This they could not agree to. I spent a couple of days considering my position and decided it would be hypocritical of me, as an ambassador for the bid, to continue drawing a salary from an organisation who could possibly have done irreparable damage to the bid. I therefore decided to resign.

I never thought my resignation would have the repercussions it did have in terms of media interest. On the plus side, it managed to galvanise a bit of support for the bid, which was what we needed to bounce back quickly from any damage the story might have done. Was it a little foolish on his part to be so loose-tongued? All I would say is that I don't think any of us have private conversations – which he thought this was – in which we don't from time to time say something that if it came out in a newspaper would be either ridiculed or get us into serious trouble, even if it's just hearsay and rumour. We've all done it.

Having said that, the things he uttered seemed slightly ridiculous, but he obviously said them without ever dreaming they would land up in the public domain. He had heard this rumour and just repeated it in confidentiality to someone he trusted. As I have said, if this had been genuine investigative journalism in the public interest, I would have had no complaints, but in this particular instance I don't think it could be justified. The newspaper made a mistake and I'm glad to say the story was widely condemned. It was a shame because I really enjoyed working for the *Mail on Sunday*, but I just felt it was a stand I had to make. I had a lot of positive feedback as a result, but I didn't do it to become a martyr. I did it because I thought it was the right thing to do.

It's difficult to say just how damaging it has been to our bid. If it had happened a week before the voting, obviously it would have been catastrophic – it never looks good when your bid committee chairman has to stand down. And it would certainly have been more damaging if Lord Triesman hadn't promptly resigned and if the bid committee hadn't quickly distanced themselves from his comments. Only the FIFA executive committee will know how damaging it has been. You just have to hope that these intelligent people understand the way in which these comments were made. I hope it won't have any lasting effect because we have a very, very strong bid with many facets and attributes. We just need to keep drumming that home.

All of this was for the future. What mattered now was that we held a World Cup – aloft.

7

The American dream is England's nightmare

After Rio Ferdinand's late withdrawal, I guess we have all had enough of late cancellations just recently, but fortunately the British Airways strike didn't affect my afternoon flight from Heathrow to Cape Town. I travelled in the company of my BBC colleague and good friend Alan Hansen. We spent much of the flight talking about the tactics that Fabio Capello might employ at this World Cup and hoped above all that he would have the good sense to play Steven Gerrard in an advanced role just behind Wayne Rooney.

When we arrived, we met up with another of the BBC's

resident analysts, former England striker Alan Shearer, and the topic was raised again. All three of us were of the opinion that this was the way for England to go, otherwise we risked becoming predictable and less effective. We just couldn't envisage England winning the World Cup with a 4–4–2 formation. Not only would Capello get the best out of Rooney and Gerrard by playing that way, but it would also enable him to stiffen the midfield, which he would have to do when England came up against the better sides of this World Cup.

I was hoping I would have the opportunity in the days and weeks ahead to get into Capello on this subject in an interview, by satellite link perhaps, providing he felt his English was up to it. With something like thirty games to cover in the first twenty-odd days, I wasn't going to get the chance to travel to England's training camp at Rustenburg to do an interview in person. I wasn't particularly optimistic about him agreeing to it. If he deployed the tactic against the United States in the opening match the idea was redundant, anyway.

The sports pages today had been full of stories about the bad language Rooney had used towards the referee in England's final warm-up game against local side Platinum Star and of the implications any repetition of that behaviour might have for England in the World Cup. But it probably wasn't so much Rooney's colourful language that concerned the England players as the scathing words of the England manager about their performance at half time. John Terry said he had never seen him so angry. What with that and the noise from the vuvuzelas during the match, their ears must have been ringing.

Wednesday 9 June

We took our first look at the new studio, about which there has been so much fuss in the newspapers back home because of its cost. All I would say is: it looks fantastic and provides a wonderful backdrop to the World Cup. I'm sure the viewers will appreciate it because it will help make them feel they are here. What more quintessential view of South Africa could you want than Table Mountain? Besides, there wasn't somewhere we could have chosen that would have enabled us to do every game from inside the stadium. It's like if you put together a football team, you want to get the best possible team and the best facilities you can in order to provide the best possible entertainment for your paying public. We just wanted to produce the best-looking pictures for our public.

I spent most of the day filming, on Table Mountain, Lion's Head and the beaches around Cape Town, doing opening links for the programme on Friday. Meanwhile, Mark Lawrenson went off to Durban to do a feature about the Boer War, and in particular about a famous hilltop battle that became known as the Battle of Spion Kop. Apparently, that's where the famous end at Anfield gets its name, so who better to do it than Lawro.

England will be big on ITV in the first week and then after that it's basically ours. I just hope their race isn't run by then, or Rooney won't be the only one cursing his misfortune. Apparently, the match officials for the England game against the United States – who are Brazilian – have been given a list of

English swearwords, so Rooney had better mind his Ps and Qs otherwise he'll be getting his M and O – Marching Orders. I find the story a bit hard to believe – I mean, are Brazilians really going to understand his Scouse accent?

All players have got to be mindful of that sort of thing, they've got to be disciplined; you don't want to pick up yellow cards for something as unnecessary as that. It might be easy for me to say, since I never once got booked as a player, but it's just that I think football's a hard enough game to play when you're fully focused, let alone when you're remonstrating and ranting at people. It's invariably a result of weakness, when things aren't going well. I wonder whether the officials will be learning swearwords in Arabic or Dutch or whatever. Probably not. Severe abuse of a referee by a player should be punished anyway, whatever the language.

It was the photographers, rather than the match officials, who were getting a tongue-lashing over at England's training camp – from Capello rather than Rooney. One of the snappers' long-range lenses – by pure chance, of course – had strayed in the direction of the building which houses the England treatment rooms, a particularly private place in their set-up just now, so Fabio snapped. 'Why are you taking these pictures, why? You're not in the UK now,' he was heard to tell one photographer. It was nothing out of the ordinary. I saw Bobby Robson lose his cool with the press photographers on more than one occasion. I don't think it was a sign that Capello was either losing the plot or laying down his authority. It was more a case of standing up for his players and engendering a bit of team spirit. As we all know, he's not a man to be trifled with.

We're hearing a lot of complaints about the Adidas Jabulani ball that they are going to be using here, which is not unusual in itself at a World Cup; keepers always moan about the characteristics of a new ball. But I've never heard so many outfield players complain before. I understand Joe Cole thinks it takes the skill out of the game, while Capello simply refers to it as the 'terrible, terrible Jabulani', making it sound like a character out of a *Stars Wars* film. We'll have to keep an eye on it during the early games just in case it becomes a factor. Bring back the old leather ones, that's what I say. Once they get the laces from one of those flush in their face they'll soon stop their whingeing!

Thursday 10 June

Looking ahead to the BBC's match between Uruguay and France tomorrow evening, I suspect there might be an upset there because there is unrest in the French camp. There was a bit of a contretemps between Chelsea's Florent Malouda and the manager Raymond Domenech. Malouda had to be physically restrained by William Gallas, so there must be a doubt about whether he'll be in the starting line-up. The players already know Domenech will be leaving after the World Cup. I don't see that as a problem, though, as some are claiming.

At Italia '90 we knew that Bobby Robson would be going. Bobby got some stick for announcing that he would be joining PSV Eindhoven after the tournament, but the Football Association had already made it clear he wouldn't be staying on as England manager and a man has to find alternative employment. It doesn't have any relevance to how the team will perform at the finals because managers are professional enough to continue doing their job properly and the players want success, if only for selfish reasons. It clearly didn't affect our performance because that was England's best at a World Cup on foreign soil.

Players are largely oblivious to outside issues when they are at a World Cup. It may be football's biggest shop window, but all that players care about is giving everything to the cause and winning. World Cups are what they dream about. It doesn't matter how much they earn or who they might be joining after the World Cup, it's a complete irrelevance.

The atmosphere here is every bit as enthusiastic as it was in Germany four years ago, but obviously very different. A ball hasn't been kicked yet, but I sense we are going to remember the vuvuzela – the horn instrument that they blow anywhere and at any time – for a very long while. The South African people are clearly thrilled to be staging this World Cup. It's evident in every face you see in the stadiums, the fan parks and on every street corner. They're immersing themselves in it totally. I'm just keeping my fingers crossed everything goes well for them tomorrow in terms of event organisation and how their team plays.

South Africa 1 Mexico 1
Uruguay 0 France 0

News of the death of Nelson Mandela's great-granddaughter in a car accident cast a shadow over the opening day of this World Cup: how incredibly sad and unfortunate. As a result, the great man wasn't able to make his anticipated appearance at the opening celebrations or indeed the opening match between South Africa and Mexico at the Soccer City Stadium in Johannesburg. We can only hope he will be well enough to make an appearance at the final. In his absence, the 91-year-old former president sent a recorded message to the thousands present and Jacob Zuma, the president, told the audience: 'He had wanted to come to greet you before the start of the match, but unfortunately there was a tragedy in the Mandela family. But he said we must enjoy the game. As a country we are humbled by this honour to host one of the biggest tournaments in the world. The time for Africa has come.'

Nor, unfortunately, was it the country's only tragedy. Mandela had requested that Siphiwo Ntshebe, a 34-year-old opera singer, perform at the opening celebrations, but he died from meningitis last month. The crowd had been instructed by Mandela to enjoy the game and that, I'm pleased to say, they did – and so did the rest of us. It finished in an immensely enjoyable 1–1 draw, and so very nearly had the perfect ending – a South African victory – when, in the closing minutes, Katiego

Mphela hit a post. Had that gone in, I imagine all present would have suffered permanent deafness as a result of the vuvuzelas. As it was, it had a cracking goal from the midfielder Siphiwe Tshabalala to savour. Rafa Marquez had levelled the game for Mexico with nine minutes remaining. So the reputation of host nations remained intact: none has ever lost an opening game. So, too, did Mexico's; they've never won one.

There was a wonderful atmosphere all over the country. The stadiums in both Johannesburg and Cape Town were vibrant, colourful and, of course, very noisy. And both matches went off without a hitch. All the concerns that people had about South Africa staging the event quickly disappeared. And if the vuvuzela players could only run out of puff or at least decline from blowing the thing as early as six o'clock in the morning – when they finished blowing it only four hours earlier – it would be much appreciated. There is talk of the instrument being banned, which I don't agree with because this is the sound of South Africa. It's also been suggested that they could be construed as a dangerous weapon. If they can ban umbrellas, as they have done at the Rustenburg stadium, they can certainly ban vuvuzelas. But far from stopping the fans from taking them into the stadium, I just wish they would be prevented from taking them out of the stadium!

All in all, it was a great first day for Africa on the occasion of their first World Cup. There's also now a real hope that South Africa can avoid the indignity and disappointment of elimination in the group stages, which would be a great achievement for the host nation.

That view was further endorsed by the performance of France and Uruguay, the BBC's opening match this evening. Unfortunately for us and the viewers, this was not France '98 revisited and the two sides played out a fairly negative goalless draw. This is the thing with World Cup television programmes: you're really only as good as your game. The best programmes invariably involve the best matches, partly because there's more of a buzz in the studio among the guests and the resident analysts, so there's more to talk about. I'm glad we invited Emmanuel Adebayor along for the South Africa game because he obviously brought with him a passion for African football. You could see how proud he was.

Presenting is not that difficult, providing it all goes smoothly. It's when there's a glitch that you have to earn your corn. I love all that sort of seat-of-your-pants stuff; it gets the adrenaline flowing. You can plan your programme and write all the clever opening lines you like, but you're largely dictated to by events on the field – in this case a bit of a non-event.

As expected, Malouda didn't make the starting line-up, which was ridiculous – disciplinary reasons apart. He was arguably Chelsea's best player last season. Instead, Domenech went with Franck Ribery on the left – which is not his natural flank – and the fairly inept Sidney Govou on the right. It was hardly surprising that when Malouda eventually joined the proceedings in the second half he was France's best player. On this evidence, the runners-up from 2006 could be making a premature exit from this World Cup, unless they sort themselves out.

Bloody-minded or not, at least Domenech knows world-class

talent when he sees it – I think. He offered an extraordinary eulogy to our own Wayne Rooney, of whom he said: 'He's my idol, a player who makes me feel just like a fan whenever I watch him. It's like I'm in the stands with a scarf around my neck, shouting *Allez Rooney!* He's got great technique and he always delivers an end result. He's the centre-forward everyone dreams of having in their side.'

Did you hear that Fabio? He calls him a centre-forward, not a second striker or an inside-forward but a No. 9. However, something told me that the England manager wasn't listening to either Domenech or the groundswell of opinion among the current players, past players and managers whom I had come into contact with since arriving in South Africa. And that was that he must play Rooney as the main striker on his own in attack, with close support from either Gerrard or Joe Cole. The word from the Royal Bafokeng sports complex in Rustenburg was that he would persist with Rooney and Heskey up front in a 4–4–2 formation against the United States tomorrow. Our mole in the England camp 'reliably' informed us that his line-up would be: Green; Johnson, King, Terry, A. Cole; Lennon, Carrick, Lampard, Gerrard; Rooney and Heskey.

Mindful of how Harold Wilson had been quick to associate himself with England's success in '66 – they were even kitted out in Labour red, according to Wilson – the prime minister David Cameron had earlier in the day respectfully referred to the Italian as 'the most important man in England'. I just hope he is backing a winner. In his retro Umbro tracksuit, which has been designed to look like the one Alf Ramsey wore, Capello, too, is harking back to '66 and like Ramsey he is giving nothing away. Snippets of information have to be dissected before anything tangible can be deduced. In his press conference today he has said that James Milner, after several days of virus problems, is fit to start, which probably means our mole has been burrowing in the wrong hole: no place for Michael Carrick then.

Gareth Barry apparently came through the day's training session impressively, although Capello has already stated quite firmly that he won't play him against the States, so it looks as if Milner will be appearing somewhere in the midfield. As for who the goalkeeper will be it's anyone's guess. Rob Green is the man in possession; David James is the man in possession of the No. 1 jersey; and Joe Hart is the man – or more to the point, the rookie – in the possession of form. Personally, I fancy he will go with the not-so-green Green.

If only some of Capello's confidence could rub off on the players, who may have lost some since the injury to Ferdinand. 'That's all that matters to me: to win and get to the final,' he said after training. 'The challenge is to win. Anything else is just words. We have to win. No more. In my mind, we play to win. That's all. I exist to win.'

With such positive thinking in their corner, England must surely be good enough to beat the USA whatever the formation, whatever Rooney's role – but where have we heard those sentiments before? We know what to expect from the Americans. They've got this work ethic, they're well organised and they've got an excellent spirit. Say what you like about the Confederations Cup, but that victory by the States over Spain in the semi-finals last summer has to be taken seriously. No one likes surrendering a winning run, never mind a world record-making run, and Spain had won 15 on the trot up until then and were unbeaten in 35 matches. They've got decent individuals right through the team, but no great individual talent. Yet somehow their manager Bob Bradley has got them functioning as a unit, which is more than can be said for some of the world's more illustrious sides. Apart from possibly their goalkeeper Tim Howard, I don't think any of their players would make the England squad.

It's time England rolled up their sleeves, got out there and gave a good performance. It's been a while since they did. I don't expect many goals, first games are nearly always cautious affairs. In fact, the only time I can remember England getting off to a flier was at Spain '82 against France, when we won 3–1 with Bryan Robson scoring after 27 seconds, which was then the fastest goal ever scored in World Cup finals.

A draw would not be a disaster so long as the performance was respectable and even then that can improve, sometimes out of all proportion, as a World Cup story unfolds. We started with a draw, against the Republic of Ireland, in 1990, but that was of some concern only because our next match was against the Netherlands. England's next match is against Algeria, which, with all due respect to Algeria, is slightly different. So there would be no reason to panic should it finish all square – defeat doesn't bear thinking about – it's just that it would help relax everyone if we could get off to a flying start or at least a winning one.

I just hope we haven't put the mockers on England by running a feature tonight on the BBC about England's infamous defeat to the US in the 1950 World Cup in Belo Horizonte. There were some charming interviews with some of the survivors from that game, particularly the American ones. I love the way one of them spoke when describing a packed penalty area: 'There was a lot of traffic in the box,' he said. Let's hope there's a lot of 'traffic' in the Americans' box tomorrow.

Saturday 12 June

South Korea 2 Greece 0
Argentina 1 Nigeria 0
England 1 USA 1

For Belo Horizonte read the Royal Bafokeng Stadium. After what happened tonight, the BBC could be making programmes sixty years from now about another team of England 'world-beaters' who got their comeuppance from the Yanks. God help us if they ever start taking this game seriously. We may not have lost on this occasion, but it certainly felt like it. Unlike 1950, this result was almost to be expected. In fact, it was as predictable as the way we played.

That as a nation we were almost apoplectic about one goalkeeping gaffe says everything you need to know about the state of our game at the moment. Do you think Brazil in 1958, 1962, 1970, 1994 or 2002 feared the worst when their goalkeeper dropped an isolated clanger, as they often did, particularly in the early days? Of course they didn't, they just went straight down the other end and made amends – usually a few times. But for England you felt it was terminal when Green allowed a 'wicked' Jabulani ball – although fairly gently struck by Clint Dempsey – to bounce off the palms of his gloves and trickle tantalisingly over the goal-line. I would like to be able to say that the Jabulani did a nasty left turn at the last moment, but several re-runs of the goal showed that while the ball bounced a couple of times there was no deviation in its route.

Green, though, wasn't responsible for this adverse result, the tactics were. I've said it many times before, when we play 4–4–2 we're easy to play against and we find it difficult to keep the ball. We've got to fill the midfield more, because that will force us to play more football. And also we need to play with pace. After all, a 1–1 draw is not a disaster, although the way we played was. We can recover from this, but Capello needs to start deploying sensible tactics.

Gerrard's goal was a perfect example of how effective we can be when he is playing in forward areas. The last place you want him is near your back four. Scoring after four minutes, à la Bryan Robson '82, could not have been better for England. It began with a quick throw-in from Glen Johnson, which the Americans were slow to react to. Then Frank Lampard found Heskey and his first-time diagonal ball was read perfectly by Gerrard. How many times have we seen him move on to a ball like that for Liverpool? And you knew the moment he steered it with the outside of his foot, as Howard committed himself, where that ball would end up.

It was a classic Gerrard goal, and one that Capello must take note of. I know he is going to say that that is the kind of position he wants to see Gerrard in, but he is more likely to be found in that position if he is located there in the first place. I just hope Capello doesn't become stubborn over this and persist in playing Gerrard as a holding midfield player or even wide on the left, because the weight of opinion about where Gerrard should play, not to mention the evidence, is heavily against him. You cannot play old-style 4–4–2 and expect to do well nowadays, it's as simple as that.

Ironically, Emile Heskey, who is the player Capello needs to stand down, was one of our few successes. Johnson was another. Emile is what he is. He won a lot in the air, held the ball up reasonably well and used his strength to batter the American defence early on. The trouble is it encourages England to whack it up to him and the consequence is that you don't keep anything like enough possession. We can get away with it in this group, but as soon as we start playing against the better teams – assuming we get that far – we're going to have big problems. Needless to say, when Heskey did get his one and only chance to score, he scorned it.

This problem of possession most crucially affects Rooney, our best player. When he doesn't see enough of the ball, he comes deep looking for it – sometimes with dangerous intent. He stayed up in attack early on, but when he found he wasn't getting the ball he became frustrated and then we lost him as a focal point. He's got to stay up there because it gives England their best out. It also forces us to play more along the wings.

A few of us in the studio had remarked on how tense Green looked in the tunnel beforehand. We were watching the world feed and I don't think he moved a muscle for all of ten minutes. Now you can look at that two ways: either he was focusing totally on the job in hand or he was petrified. Perhaps he always looks that way before going out to play for West Ham, but I fancy not. It must have been difficult for him to continue after the calamity and I'm glad for his sake, if not England's, that Capello didn't replace him at half time. As it turned out, he went on to make a vital, if somewhat fortuitous, save from Jozy Altidore, which his captain kindly said afterwards more than made amends for his mistake. It didn't, of course.

It was the kind of blunder that can happen to anyone, but you just cannot let it happen at a World Cup. World Cups can make or break you and, sadly, this error has probably broken Green. Having said that, he had the courage to come out and face the media afterwards, which many men wouldn't have done. But no amount of bravery will prevent this error from haunting him, probably forever.

I thought of Peter Bonetti and the mistake he made in the 1970 World Cup quarter-final against West Germany – or at least the only one he would admit to – when he allowed Franz Beckenbauer's fairly feeble shot from the edge of the area to beat him. He said he had run that goal through his mind thousands of times and that one of these days he would save it. Green will at least have to try to erase the hurt if he is to move on, but it won't be easy. Ideally, he needs to begin the erasure here, but whether Capello will give him the opportunity, I somehow doubt it. For the time being, at least, I fear he is fatally scarred. This will finish his World Cup, I'm sure.

To be fair to the Americans, they were probably worthy of their equaliser at the time. We failed to build on our early goal. We seemed to sit back and hand the initiative to the Americans. When we did attack we had chances to score because the States looked so weak defensively, but the final ball too often let us down. Lennon clearly had the beating of his full-back, as he does most full-backs, but just didn't seem to have sufficient belief in himself to get to the byline and make the cross. Milner may have recovered from his stomach bug, but he clearly wasn't match fit, as was evident from one late tackle that could have earned him a booking. At least Capello saw that early enough and after half an hour substituted him, bringing on Shaun Wright-Phillips.

If the reappearance of Green for the second half was a slight concern to some, it was nothing compared to the non-reappearance of King because of a groin strain. They say the Tottenham central defender is a Rolls-Royce among defenders. If he is, then his replacement, Jamie Carragher, is the equivalent of a Volkswagen Beetle: reliable but not a lot of speed. Worse still, he had the one-paced John Terry alongside him. Was England's worst nightmare about to be realised? As it turned out, Carragher got done for pace just once – and it almost proved fatal.

It was probably just as well that he had a yellow card hanging over him, when Altidore broke away down the left wing in the 65th minute, otherwise he might have been inclined to do more than just lean heavily on the American. Wisely, or unwisely as it may have seemed at the time, he chose to leave his fate and that of England to Green, who partially redeemed himself by thrusting out a strong hand to the former Hull striker's shot. Luck in the shape of an obstinate post did the rest.

How Green could have done with the Hand of God. Trust Diego Maradona to rub salt in our wounds. Earlier in the day, after South Korea had comfortably beaten the 2004 European champions Greece with goals from Jung-Soo Lee and Manchester United's Ji-Sung Park, his Argentina side had played Nigeria and after all that we had heard about his bizarre squad selection policy and even more bizarre preparations, the former world champions seemed ripe for a fall. We should have known better. Argentina were positively inspired by the animated little figure in a large shiny grey suit on the touchline. You could tell he was just desperate to join in on the pitch, so much so I've never seen a more willing ball-boy. The end result – which was much closer than it should have been – was that his alter ego Lionel Messi finally transferred his club form to the international stage. He would have scored at least a couple but for a combination of superb goalkeeping by Vincent Enyeama and finishing that was, dare one say, almost Heskeyesque. As it was, Argentina had to make do with a pile-driver of a header from Gabriel Heinze. So a good day for Manchester United boys, old and new – but not Rooney.

Venue:	Royal Bafokeng Stadium, Rustenburg
Attendance:	38,646
England:	Green; Johnson, Terry, King (Carragher, HT), A. Cole; Lennon, Lampard, Gerrard, Milner (Wright-Phillips 31); Rooney, Heskey (Crouch 79)
Scorer:	Gerrard (4)
Yellow card:	Milner (26), Carragher (60), Gerrard (61)
USA:	Howard; Cherundolo, DeMerit, Onyewu, Bocanegra; Donovan, Bradley, Clark, Dempsey; Findley (Buddle 77), Altidore (Holden 86)
Scorer:	Dempsey (40)
Yellow card:	Cherundolo (6), DeMerit (15), Findley (20)
Shots:	England 8/18, USA 4/13
Possession:	England 54%, USA 46%
Referee:	Carlos Simon (Brazil)

121

8

Fear of failure

Algeria 0 Slovenia 1

Serbia 0 Ghana 1

Germany 4 Australia 0

It must have been a while since American sports pages contained headlines about horizontal British heavyweights – never mind Dempsey winning by a KO – but they were entitled to gloat after last night's acutely embarrassing performance by England against the United States. The British media seemed to lay most of the blame at the hands of Fabio Capello rather than the butterfingers of Robert Green, which seemed about right. After all, the England goalkeeper made just one mistake, whereas the manager made a few.

Comfortably the most glaring were his tactical mistakes. His refusal to play Steven Gerrard in a more central, attacking role is a mystery to even some of his one-time disciples like Marcel Desailly and Clarence Seedorf, who are among the BBC's team of pundits here in South Africa. His loyalty to Emile Heskey, an honest but unproductive striker, is misguided, and other decisions he took over players of questionable fitness backfired. Apparently, Ledley King was telling John Terry that his groin felt tight not long after England's fourth-minute goal; while James Milner, only just recovered from a stomach virus, clearly wasn't match fit. And, finally, of course, it was Capello's decision to go with Green ahead of the more experienced David James, who, by the way, claims he was fit enough to play.

Worse still, there came news from the England camp today that King will be out at least until the quarter-finals of this tournament. It's a devastating blow, coming so soon after the loss of Rio Ferdinand, but quite frankly, like Ferdinand, not one that will surprise anyone greatly. King was always a risk. The question is: was he a risk worth taking? To be fair to Capello, he didn't have too many options. He was obviously hoping that, between them, Ferdinand and King could cater for England's needs, but instead he has ended up losing both of them through injury. As if by magic, English centre-backs, much like English goalkeepers, have suddenly disappeared off the face of the earth.

Seedorf suggested that we are all getting a bit too negative. So looking at the positives, I would say England can recover from this miserable start, just as the England teams I played for at Mexico '86 and Italia '90 did when we also started disappointingly – with a defeat in the case of 1986. The difference then was that we created many more chances against Portugal than the class of 2010 did. I suppose we shouldn't have been too surprised: the three warm-up games weren't convincing, even if we did win them. Very few teams hit the ground running in World Cups, most start edgily, and I still fully expect England and our friends from across the Atlantic to qualify from Group C.

In the cold light of day, I still don't see how Capello can play Green in the next match, as much as I would like him to for Green's own salvation. As I have said before, you only find out how good a keeper is when he has a howler. If this were the Premier League, you would say he has to get straight back up on the horse that threw him, but is the World Cup the place to find out what Green is made of? One more clanger and England could possibly be out. My BBC colleague Alan Hansen thought Capello should have taken him off at half time, but I'm glad Capello didn't because it gave him the opportunity to atone partially.

Alan Shearer remarked on how opponents would seize on any perceived weakness of England, while Lee Dixon was more concerned about the negative effect it would have upon the back four – as he would! We haven't kept just one clean sheet in ten games now. One thing's for sure, whomever Capello chooses, if it goes wrong he'll be pilloried. He's got to make his decision and then sit on the touchline and pray.

Credit Green, though, for facing the music after the game and even bringing a touch of light relief to the sombre mood when he told the press he had been called up for a random drugs test and 'no, they didn't find any performance-enhancing drugs'.

We need a shot of something, though, to lift our spirits – perhaps the anticipated return of Gareth Barry for the match against Algeria will do it. Never has a Steady-Eddie type been so sorely missed as Barry; he seems to have become a key player without even kicking a ball. But, by sitting in front of the back four, he will enable Frank Lampard and Gerrard to get forward more, which is of paramount importance. Even though he is used in a more attacking position by his club – the Dutchman Nigel de Jong performs the minding duties at Manchester City – he has carried out the holding role effectively for Capello. My only concern is that, as with King and Milner, he may not be sufficiently fit after six weeks out through injury. He can hardly be expected to find his form immediately. At least games against the likes of Algeria and Slovenia shouldn't be too demanding.

King's injury leaves us with absolutely no pace at the heart of defence if Capello turns to Jamie Carragher, as I'm sure he will. If he had any confidence in Michael Dawson and Matthew Upson, he would have used them in the pre-tournament friendlies. Instead, he called back the old stager from Liverpool who retired a couple of years ago. Upson is left-sided, the same as Terry, and Dawson has pace only once he gets going. I think I would go for youth and try the Tottenham player, but it's not ideal. That little triangle between goalkeeper and central defenders is so important to a team's stability and ours is beginning to look more like the Bermuda Triangle.

In 1986 I remember we were outnumbered in midfield by the Portuguese, which is what I think is going to happen to us here unless Capello rethinks his tactics. Bobby Robson bolstered the midfield and made a change up front after our second game, a goalless draw with Morocco, and our fortunes changed dramatically with a 3–0 win against Paraguay. In 1990, after a dire 1–1 draw against the Republic of Ireland, he made more of a fundamental tactical change for our second game, against the Netherlands, by introducing a sweeper system for the first time in his England managerial career. Unlike the present England manager, Bobby was spoiled for choice at centre-back, with three outstanding individuals in Terry Butcher, Mark Wright and Des Walker. Walker was rapid. How the current England side could do with his kind of pace. In World Cups, fortune often favours the brave and Capello – who, for all his experience, is, after all, a rookie when it comes to World Cups – would do well to remember that.

'This is how we've got to play international football from now on,' said my old mate Peter Shilton at the time. It wasn't, but the tactics were right at the time. The game evolves, but the bottom line is you must play people in their natural positions – the game's hard enough without playing out of position – and Gerrard is far more comfortable in a central, forward position than sat in front of the back four or marginalised out on the left wing.

The Americans might be improving as an international side, but their knowledge of the game still leaves something to be desired, as was evident from the headline in the *New York Post*, which read 'USA wins 1–1'. Nevertheless, you have to applaud the positive attitude of their media, which contrasts somewhat with ours.

It transpired that Green's monumental gaffe wasn't the only one last night. Our opposition, ITV, made one, too. Moments before Gerrard's goal, their HD coverage suddenly cut to an advert for Hyundai for a few seconds and 1.5 million viewers missed England's only high point of the match. I can assure you that, just like the substitute goalkeepers on the England bench when Green blundered, none of us at the BBC was smirking because that kind of misfortune can befall anyone. Even so, it was extraordinary that that sort of thing should be happening to them a second time. During their coverage of an FA Cup tie between Everton and Liverpool last year their picture cut to a Tic-Tac advert a split-second before Everton's winner. Even Hansen would not have welcomed that. Well, maybe …

Green's spirits and those of England will have been lifted marginally by a goalkeeping error of similar magnitude to the England keeper's in Algeria's 1–0 defeat to Slovenia. However, Algeria's first 'own goal' was to have substitute Abdelkader Ghezzal sent off for two yellow cards received in record time. The Slovenian player Robert Koren then hit the sort of shot that his team-mates might have chided him about afterwards had it not skipped through the hands of Faouzi Chaouchi. At least Green is a good keeper 99 per cent of the time; I'm not sure the same could be said of Chaouchi. England ought to have been cheered by how poor both sides looked.

There was another sending-off in the mid-afternoon match between Ghana and Serbia, when the latter's Aleksandar Lukovic received two yellow cards. Although the only goal of the game came eight minutes later through a penalty by Asamoah Gyan, which was controversially awarded, Ghana were good value for the victory, Africa's first of the competition. Capello will need to keep his eye on the Black Stars, who are possible opponents in the round of 16. You would have thought they had already won the World Cup, judging by the way Fulham's John Pantsil was parading his country's flag around the pitch afterwards.

Trust Germany to announce their arrival in rather more emphatic fashion than England. Their 4–0 win against Australia brought some much-needed excitement to the competition and, just as importantly, goals. Until their four-goal hit, we were almost a goal a game down compared to 2006. Their performance singled them out as unexpected title contenders, not that a Germany side is ever really that at a World Cup. Even though the scoreline, on this occasion, may have been influenced by a sending-off – Everton's Tim Cahill was harshly treated, I thought, by Mexican referee Marco Rodriguez – it was an impressive performance and one that slightly surprised the BBC's guest pundit Jürgen Klinsmann.

Looking young enough still to have been selected himself, England's favourite German hadn't expected quite so much so soon from this young German side, containing, as it does, four or five members of the Under-21 side which won the UEFA Championship in Sweden last summer, outclassing England in the final. Among those who took the eye was Mesut Özil, a player of Turkish parentage whose goal extinguished England's hopes in Malmö. He seemed to be pulling the strings just behind our old friend Miroslav Klose, who scored, typically with a header, to go above me in the list for international goals as well as World Cup ones. Lukas Podolski started the rout and Thomas Müller and Cacau completed it. Interestingly, Klose has scored only one goal outside the group stages of a World Cup.

They weren't the only ones with something to celebrate. It was Hansen's 55th birthday and, the generous Jock that he is, he treated us all to dinner at a magnificent seafood restaurant.

Monday 14 June

Netherlands 2 Denmark 0

Japan 1 Cameroon 0

Italy 1 Paraguay 1

Talk about kicking a man when he is down. Franz Beckenbauer, the respectable face of German football for so many years, has accused England of going backwards and playing 'kick and rush'. He said we had reverted to football of a bygone age – and I have to say, looking at England's performance against the United States, he has a point. When we play with a big man up front, it tends to encourage that kind of football and there was a lot of long ball up to Heskey. There was also too big a gap between our defenders and our forwards; we weren't compact enough.

Capello's quite a stubborn individual. You have to be in order to become a successful manager. You have to be strong and make your own decisions. But you cannot afford to be inflexible and unreceptive to change, and I'm beginning to think that's what Capello is. We're always a bit hyper-critical about the England team, but that's because we care so much about our football. I'm sure the fans of most of the other countries at this World Cup are equally concerned about their teams right now: Italy looked pretty average in their 1–1 draw with Paraguay; the Netherlands were lethargic until a fortuitous Daniel Agger own goal got them going in their 2–0 win against Denmark – Liverpool's Dirk Kuyt added a second late on; and France the other day were pretty awful.

Everyone expects their team to come out and play staggering football right away, but it generally doesn't work like that in major tournaments – certainly not in the first round of games when the onus is on teams not to lose rather than having to win. Oddly enough, the last World Cup in Germany bucked that trend, because it started terrifically with some great games and then fear crept in and it petered out in the knockout stages. Marcello Lippi, the Italian manager, didn't seem too concerned judging by his comment: 'I'm very satisfied with our performance. The only thing I regret is normally matches of this type, we win.' They might have lost it had the Paraguay keeper Justo Villar not completely missed Simone Pepe's corner in the 64th minute, which allowed Daniele De Rossi a tap-in. Before then, Wigan had been on course to have a hand in the Azzurri's defeat when Antolin Alcaraz, their recent free transfer, took advantage of an uncharacteristic lapse by Fabio Cannavaro and co to head Paraguay in front.

The Kaiser also said there was a lack of quality in the England team, which Capello could do little about. He blamed that on the profusion of foreign players in the English game. Capello himself has bemoaned the fact that less than one third of the players in the Premier League are English. I'm not sure I wholly agree with Beckenbauer about that, because I think there is quality in our team. Certainly, we need to produce more home-grown talent, and I think in the next five to ten years we will do because the academies have improved; they teach a more technical game than they used to. But it doesn't mean to say if we had more English players in the Premier League the national team would be better. It just means there would be more average players in the league who were English.

What you're seeing now are English players, who would otherwise be turning out in the Premier League, playing in the Championship. The best, the Rooneys, the Gerrards, the Lampards of this world, will always come through no matter what. I just don't get that argument that if we didn't have so many foreign players we would automatically have better English players and a better national team. Surely, the issue is that we're not producing enough quality footballers and we haven't done for quite some time.

Today's games weren't overly entertaining and, much as I'm loathe to say so, I'm wondering whether some of it's down to the peculiar characteristics of this Jabulani ball. It was supposed to produce more goals, but instead it's produced fewer. Most of the free-kicks seem to be going over the bar, crosses almost invariably fly long and it's just possible it has contributed to some of the goalkeeping errors and even maybe the handballs. It looks like a beach ball to me.

There's also a question of some countries gaining an unfair advantage, since the Germans, the Swiss, the Dutch and the Portuguese were using the ball last season in their domestic league from December onwards. Carragher said that England start off every practice session striking the ball to each other from distance to try to get used to it. England used it for the first time twelve days before the finals began in their unsightly victory over Japan in Graz. I don't suppose anything will be done about it because of sponsorship deals.

As for the other contentious instrument at these finals, one French station, I understand, is offering vuvuzela-free commentary. The Cameroon fans ought to have used them to give their manager, Paul Le Guen, a discordant blast of disapproval over his decision to play Samuel Eto'o, one of the world's great strikers, on the right wing in their 1–0 defeat to Japan. A player by the name of Honda scored the winning goal, although as far as I know there's no sponsorship deal arranged there. Le Guen's madcap decision may end up costing them.

It wasn't a great match, but at least Emmanuel Adebayor brought some light relief afterwards during the post-match analysis when his mobile phone went off, not once but twice. I said to Manu on air, 'You might want to get that,' and he looked a bit embarrassed. Shearer and I had a laugh about it, but afterwards he apologised and said that he normally had it on silent, but he was waiting for a call from his wife. I said, 'Oh, yeah.' And he said, 'Yes, we had a little girl yesterday. My wife gave birth to our first child.' My first thought was: 'You should have answered it,' and my second was: 'What on earth are you doing here in South Africa watching this dreadful match with us?' It's been good to have him on the show, he's a nice, smiley guy and he knows his stuff.

Talking of new-born, I was staggered to learn that Felipe Melo, the Brazilian midfielder, has named his son after me! He's called him Lineker. Can you believe that? Apparently, I was his father's favourite player. Of all the wonderful Brazilian names, not to mention wonderful Brazilian footballers, he could have chosen to name his son after … Zico, Socrates, Pelé. Instead, he names him after the jug-eared goal-hanger from Leicester. I was quite flattered until I heard he called his other son Dixon. Good player that Melo.

Tuesday 15 June

New Zealand 1 Slovakia 1
Ivory Coast 0 Portugal 0
Brazil 2 North Korea 1

There were stories in the British media today that James had fallen out of favour with Capello over a disagreement about his state of fitness, but I always take those kind of stories with a pinch of salt. Everyone seems to have their personal favourite among the three keepers, or should I say the one they suspect is least fallible. All three have their flaws: Hart looks reliable, but he's a rookie; Green may be psychologically damaged after the other night; and James is experienced but, as we all know, has a blunder in him waiting to happen, although possibly not on the scale of Green's. I thought the *Sun* newspaper had the best idea: on their front page they had a picture of all three standing side-by-side on the goal-line next to a headline which read, 'Capello unveils new goalie strategy'.

Green is being psychologically assessed by Christian Lattanzio, who sometimes translates for Capello. I always think that any sportsman who needs to be psychologically assessed is the type you need to worry about, but everyone's different and if it works for you I suppose that's all that matters. Some players need someone to boost their confidence, while others do it for themselves. Shilton, someone who never had that problem, has complained about a 'continuing lack of clarity' in the goalkeeping situation, which he definitely suffered from during the build-up to the 1982 World Cup, when he and Ray Clemence were alternated, which was a crazy thing to do. At least Capello hasn't done that; in fact he has gone with Green most of the time.

I'm just concerned that Green will get wind of all the 'Rob Green Jokes' that are flying around. My son George must have texted me about thirty today in one go. The English love a bit of gallows humour. Being able to laugh at yourself is a good thing, but at the same time you have to have some inner-confidence, and we don't seem to have that as a nation. When you have it, sport becomes a much easier thing to succeed at. Clint Dempsey, the scorer of the Americans' equaliser against us, seemed to suggest our whole team needed psychoanalysis, saying that even when England were ahead they seemed edgy, including the likes of Gerrard and Lampard.

The low scoring continued today with a 1–1 draw between New Zealand and Slovakia and a goalless draw between Ivory Coast and Portugal. After fourteen games, only once has there been more than two goals in a game. Arsene Wenger had said before the World Cup: 'I don't believe we're in for a feast of attacking football.' It looks as though he may be spot on. He also thought the World Cup suffered by comparison with the best of the Champions League, but that's inevitable because club teams spend far more time together than international sides and the better ones can draw their players from all over the world. Anyway, he has always put club before country.

New Zealand left it very late to get their goal – it was the third minute of injury time when Winston Reid, who had represented Denmark at Under-21 level, scored to secure New Zealand their first World Cup point. After such an historic goal, he must have been glad he threw in his lot with the Kiwis. Slovakia opened the scoring through Robert Vittek with a header which looked offside, but it was a chance missed for them and they knew it; their coach Vladimir Weiss, obviously the type who doesn't look on the bright side of life, spoke about being 'fatally wounded'.

At least it gave us the excuse to drag out some footage of Scotland's game against New Zealand in 1982, for which Dixon did a lovely analysis, whereby he managed to blame Hansen for both the Kiwis' goals. We also managed to unearth a shot from Hansen that nearly hit a corner flag. We needed some light relief as the match was not hugely attractive. In fact, it was watched by a crowd of just 23,871, the smallest at the World Cup finals since Mexico '86.

Group G, the tournament's 'Group of Death', looks like being a slow torture, judging by the cagey manner in which Ivory Coast and Portugal approached its first game. Sven-Goran Eriksson seems to have reined in that natural African ebullience, while you would never have guessed that Carlos Queiroz was indoctrinated by Manchester United, judging by the inhibition with which his Portugal team played. After hitting a post with a super effort that was very much in the United style, Cristiano Ronaldo allowed himself to be distracted by his own histrionics.

At least Brazil, we thought, would fill their boots with goals and our hearts with glee in the late kick-off against North Korea, but not a bit of it. There had been rumours that North Korean state television would not show the game if it resulted in a beating for their side, but this was one beating they could be proud of. They were disciplined and incredibly well organised until Maicon scored with a thumping goal from an outrageous angle which was very much in the best Brazilian tradition. I still haven't made up my mind whether he meant it as a cross or not, but I'm happy to give him the benefit of the doubt. He's not typically Brazilian, but he's like Cafu and Roberto Carlos in that he can get up and down that wing all day. Otherwise, it was generally a performance that reflected the dour playing style of their coach and former World Cup-winning captain Dunga. We may have to rely on Spain and Argentina to provide the flair in this World Cup.

Robinho rewarded Dunga for sticking with him during his largely hapless time at Manchester City last season with a superb virtuoso performance, which included the creation of the second Brazilian goal for another one-time Eastlands discontent, Elano. A fine and deserved 89th minute goal by Ji Yun Nam now means that perhaps Pak Doo-ik, the legendary match winner against Italy in 1966, won't be the only North Korean name anyone outside that country knows.

It will be interesting to see what happens to Robinho next season, because Roberto Mancini wants him back after his loan spell in Brazil. He didn't seem to put his heart and soul into his English career when Mark Hughes was there and caused him a few problems. He wasn't Hughes's signing, but a statement of intent by the club. It didn't prove to be a very powerful statement. Real Madrid don't tend to let great players leave the club.

All of us at the BBC here in South Africa were shocked this evening to hear that Robbie Earle has been sacked from his job as a football pundit for ITV over a World Cup ticket scandal.

Wednesday 16 June

Honduras 0 Chile 1

Spain 0 Switzerland 1

South Africa 0 Uruguay 3

Two huge disappointments today, one expected the other not. Spain, my favourites and just about everybody else's, were beaten 1–0 by Switzerland, which is comparable to Rafael Nadal losing to just about any other Swiss player but Roger Federer. In fact, I imagine Federer must have wished it had come a week later so he could have rubbed Rafa's nose in it at Wimbledon. Sadly, the host nation's 3–0 defeat to Uruguay was something we fully expected, but which most people hoped wouldn't happen, at least not this early in the competition. It has almost certainly meant they will fail to qualify for the knockout stages, which will be a bitter blow to their wonderful support. I just hope another African country can pick up the baton.

The match in Durban was just another example of how well organised some of the smaller footballing countries are nowadays. The Swiss gave a master-class in that respect. They were very clever. They played it very narrow and invited Spain to go at them from the flanks, confident in their belief that they could handle the crosses. At times all 22 players seemed to be occupying a strip down the middle of the pitch no more than 20 yards wide. At half time Vicente Del Bosque, the Spain manager, made a tactical change to try to get round the problem, but the Swiss held firm. The Swiss hoped for a draw and ended up with a scabby sort of win, courtesy of a scrambled goal by midfielder Gelson Fernandes. Spain's goalkeeper Iker Casillas didn't exactly cover himself in either glory or courage by trying to reclaim the ball with his feet instead of his hands.

Afterwards, the Real Madrid icon was interviewed on Spanish television by Sara Carbonero, who also happens to be his girlfriend. The Spanish public already think the TV presenter is a distracting influence and were further dismayed to hear her ask Casillas: 'How did you manage to muck it up?' Needless to say, he wasn't too sure how to field that one. I still think Spain will bounce back because they have so much quality, but there now exists the possibility that the two favourites – Spain and Brazil – could meet as early as the second round.

Spain may have pulled up short, but Chile didn't disappoint earlier in the day with an enthralling 1–0 victory against Honduras in which the Udinese forward Alexis Sanchez was outstanding. They were well worthy of the goal scored by Jean Beausejour and much more. It is already clear that the South Americans are in better form than the Europeans at this World Cup, and Uruguay again impressed against a South African team who were sadly out of their depth. Diego Forlan was the best player on the pitch against France and he was pretty special here, too, scoring twice despite playing in a deeper role, before Alvaro Pereira headed home a third in added time.

Looking at Forlan now, it's hard to understand how he failed to make the grade at Old Trafford. Maybe it was a bit too much for him at that stage of his career. I remember when Mark Hughes joined me at Barcelona, he found it very difficult. He was only 21 or something at the time and he went on to have a terrific career everywhere else. When you struggle to score, as Forlan did at Manchester United, the pressure can build up until it becomes intolerable.

The only news of note from the England camp was Capello's confirmation that Barry will start against Algeria – so he's made an exception there about not naming who will be playing until two hours before kick-off!

I had the distinct feeling this tournament turned the corner today as we entered the second phase of group games; just the right time then for England to come good, hopefully.

Argentina 4 South Korea 1
Greece 2 Nigeria 1
France 0 Mexico 2

My senses weren't wrong. The tournament has come to life at last: three terrific games today. Argentina were superb and Lionel Messi looked like the absolute star he is. Diego Maradona wasn't bad either in an off-field cameo role. The pair of them are pure box office. An ideal World Cup is the home nation doing well and the likes of Argentina, Brazil or maybe the Dutch turning it on on those days when the home nation isn't appearing. South Africa may not have long for this World Cup, unfortunately, but the star acts are holding their end up.

It's odd that Messi, a prolific goalscorer in club football, has yet to score here, but it's not for want of trying and only a matter of time before he does. As it was, he had a part in all four goals, Gonzalo Higuain's hat-trick and even Park Chu Young's own goal. I still think Argentina are vulnerable defensively, at right-back – Jonas Gutierrez's loss through suspension now is not a great one – and central defence, but the great thing is that like the Brazil teams of old they play to their strength, which in their case is also attack. Argentina ended up qualifying by playing a rather defensive, counter-attacking style, which didn't bring the

best out of Messi. Critics said Maradona was deliberately sub-
duing the man who would be king, because he didn't want him
to assume his mantle, but he's proved what a nonsense that was —
not that he doesn't enjoy the limelight. He's changed the tactics
to suit Messi, so good on Diego for doing so. Messi is beginning
to look like the kind of player that Maradona was in World
Cups. He has the potential to become the greatest player of all
time, or at least comparable to Maradona and Pelé.

It never ceases to amaze me how teams, after all their hard
work in qualifying, can then throw it all away in a moment of
madness. Nigeria were a goal up through Kalu Uche and in control against Greece when Sani Kaita decided to throw it all away
by needlessly lashing out a foot in the direction of Vasileios
Torosidis. Red mist was followed by red card and Greece were
soon on their way to their first World Cup goal, courtesy of
Dimitrios Salpingidis, and first World Cup win, courtesy of
Vasileios Torosidis, although he was ably assisted by the hitherto
impeccable Vincent Enyeama in the Nigeria goal.

France's wretched World Cup is practically over almost
before it has begun. You might say it's been badly handled
throughout: from their controversial winner in the play-offs
against the Republic of Ireland to their discordant, disaffected
and, some would say, thoroughly deserved 2–0 defeat here to
Mexico, in which Thierry Henry, their hero-cum-villain, appropriately had no hand. Raymond Domenech, their unloved
coach, squirmed on the touchline as goals from Javier
Hernandez and Cuauhtemoc Blanco as good as put them out of
their misery.

England, on the other hand, are not ready to go home just yet, even if, to gasps from on-lookers at training in Cape Town, Green spilled one in a not too dissimilar fashion to the one he did for real at Rustenburg. Anyway, apparently, a lot of money has been bet with William Hill on James getting the nod from Capello instead. I reckon I could go in goal against Algeria.

I don't understand all this talk about when the team should be named, although I admit it's unusual not knowing who your No. 1 keeper is. When I was at Barcelona, Johan Cruyff didn't name his team until an hour before kick-off, but you pretty much knew from training who was playing and who wasn't. It was the same with Terry Venables and most of the other managers I've played for. I don't think a player has a right to know whether he's playing or not 24 hours beforehand. The England coach explained that he was reluctant to tell his players his team the day before a match ever since he had a few bad experiences at Milan, when players subsequently pulled out through injury and he had trouble motivating their replacements.

Motivation should be the least of England's problems tomorrow night. I reckon the team will show just one change from the side that beat Croatia 5–1 at Wembley last September – Carragher for Upson – which ought to be encouragement enough. That line-up was: Green; Johnson, Terry, Upson, A. Cole; Lennon, Barry, Lampard, Gerrard; Heskey, Rooney. Of course, on that occasion we also played 4–4–2 with Gerrard in that loose position on the left. And if Rooney needs any further encouragement I can tell him that I, like him, went six internationals without scoring in 1986 and then I got three against

Poland. It's far better to score them when you really need them. And right now we need them.

Germany 0 Serbia 1
Slovenia 2 USA 2
England 0 Algeria 0

The old sign outside the dressing rooms at the Green Point Stadium read: 'Go strong or go home', but England did not take heed and as a result they may suffer the consequences. This was as bad a performance by an England team as I can remember. I have never seen them look so out of sorts and, like everyone else, I'm at a loss to understand why. How can players who perform so brilliantly in the Premier League week in, week out look so inept?

The malaise seemed to affect almost everyone, even Rooney. The Manchester United striker has not looked himself for a while, not since he injured his ankle in that Champions League quarter-final against Bayern Munich at the end of March, but rarely have I seen him look so subdued, so bereft of technique or ideas. His touch was so poor it reminded me of that film *Space Jam*, with Michael Jordan, where everyone loses their powers and behaves like amateurs.

If England never really looked like conceding a goal they certainly never looked like scoring one. They seemed incapable of shooting even when obvious opportunities presented themselves.

Instead the responsibility got passed on. They seemed gripped by the fear of failure, but then you tell yourself that this is impossible. These players are playing for some of the biggest clubs in the world in the biggest competitions in the world. How on earth can they be frightened about facing the likes of Algeria?

The only really minor surprise in his team selection was his decision to go with James, who has long been my preferred choice. It was the first time England have changed their goalkeeper during a World Cup, apart from when Peter Bonetti took Gordon Banks's place because of illness in Mexico in 1970. The Portsmouth man didn't do anything wrong and brought a stabilising presence to England's defence, as did Barry – the only player to know for certain he was playing before the day of the game – until he caught the England sickness and became as poor as everyone else.

Capello did not enjoy his 64th birthday and was as nonplussed as everyone else. 'It reminds me of when I first started as England manager; I saw the same fear when we played at Wembley,' he said. 'This is incredible given the level of the England players, but I think it is because the pressure of the World Cup is so big that the performance of the players was not so good. Yet this is the same team that more or less played most of the games in qualification for the World Cup. The problem is that the same players who were really good then are not good as a team at the moment.'

The question is how do they become cohesive again? How do they become the team they were in qualification, when many people were confidently predicting they would become world champions? Now is the time for Capello to earn his corn. He has to lift their spirits. He has to make them realise that all is not lost. Their destiny – as luck would have it – is still in their own hands. If they beat Slovenia in their final game at Nelson Mandela Bay, Port Elizabeth, next Wednesday they qualify for the knockout stages, it's as simple as that. Well, simple in theory.

If you are going to have two shocking games, I suppose it is better you have them now, when it doesn't lead to elimination. At least, not yet it doesn't. I'm clutching at straws, I know, but everyone has to remain positive – even the supporters. Perhaps, most importantly, the supporters. You could almost hear the groans of despair from back home, never mind the boos from within the stadium. If ever there was a time to get behind the England team it's now.

Some would say even our greatest player, Rooney, merited substitution, if only because of his body language: it was defeatist, which I never thought I would say of him. But you have to stick with your best players because they are the ones who will ultimately get you out of trouble. Rooney's comment in the direction of the camera afterwards, when he said, 'Nice to see your own fans booing you, you football "supporters",' was ill-advised and unfortunate but understandable in the circumstances. I for one will forgive him: I've been there. He was frustrated. But it will all be forgotten and forgiven if he scores a couple against Slovenia.

I don't know what's happened to Capello in some ways. His substitutions are usually excellent, but his first one puzzled me, because Shaun Wright-Phillips for Lennon was just like for like.

He needed someone who offered something different, someone who could rouse them from their torpor. In short, he needed Joe Cole. But like Carlo Ancelotti, he could find no room for him. Perhaps it's an Italian thing, but I really don't know what he's got against him. It's the same with the idea of Gerrard playing behind Rooney. Almost to a man, everyone agrees it's the only way to go if we are to salvage this campaign, but Capello refuses to see it. And, of course, if he does do it now it may be seen as a climb-down. Personally, I would see it as a brave decision on the part of the manager. Afterwards he said: 'I can change.' Well, prove it.

For one thing, it would stop us hitting that damn ball long and force us to play through the middle. In effect, to pass the thing! If the Jabulani ball could speak it would be telling him this: 'If you hit me long I'll just float away – like your dreams.' I bought one yesterday and it's little more than a beach ball, a plastic-coated thing, like one of those balls you see on the sea front selling at £1.99.

I don't like to keep banging on about it, but there are parallels with 1986 and 1990. At both World Cups it was obvious that Robson had to change things. In 1986 he could have taken me out, but instead chose to remove Mark Hateley. Peter Beardsley was promoted to the team and placed in that hole between midfield and attack, the same area I and many others would like to see Gerrard in, and suddenly it just clicked. In 1990 we changed the system and proved that English players can pass the ball. In both instances, we hit on a winning formula. It can happen to this England team, but it must happen now.

It's certainly a weird tournament. Who would have predicted that Spain, Italy, France, England and even Germany today would struggle. At least Germany could claim extenuating circumstances in the case of their 1–0 defeat to Serbia after Klose was sent off for receiving two yellow cards, the first of which was quite absurd. Even with ten men, they were better than Serbia until eventually succumbing to a goal from Milan Jovanovic.

Thankfully, the United States were cruelly denied a victory at the death against Slovenia by Malian referee Koman Coulibaly, who inexplicably failed to allow a 'goal' by Maurice Edu when half a dozen American players could claim they were being fouled in the box. Slovenia played quite well to go 2–0 up, through goals by Valter Birsa and Zlatan Ljubijankic, and then nearly threw it all away with some awful defending to let in Landon Donovan and Michael Bradley. If we can't beat Slovenia we should be walking home not flying home.

Venue:	Green Point Stadium, Cape Town
Attendance:	64,100
England:	James; Johnson, Carragher, Terry, A. Cole; Lennon (Wright-Phillips 63), Barry (Crouch 84), Lampard, Gerrard; Heskey (Defoe 74), Rooney
Yellow card:	Carragher (58)
Algeria:	Bolhi; Kadir, Bougherra, Yahia, Belhadj; Boudebouz (Abdoun 74), Yebda (Mesbah 88), Halliche, Lacen, Ziani (Guedioura 81); Matmour
Yellow card:	Lacen (85)
Shots:	England 6/15, Algeria 1/11
Possession:	England 48%, Algeria 52%
Referee:	Ravshan Irmatov (Uzbekistan)

That's more like it!

Netherlands 1 Japan 0

Ghana 1 Australia 1

Cameroon 1 Denmark 2

England's players were probably more appreciative of the visit from Buckingham Palace than Crystal Palace after the game. No sooner had Prince William and Prince Harry visited the England dressing room to commiserate with them than Pavlos Joseph – apparently looking for the toilet – wandered in to have a few words with the boys. 'You are a disgrace,' the Greek Cypriot son of SE25 fish-and-chip-shop proprietors told them, which, to be fair, was probably the view of the entire nation. I was just amazed this England fan got into the dressing room. Less amazed he got stuck into the team.

While I'm sure the English press would love to have reported on a great England victory against Algeria, they are still capable of enjoying themselves in moments of national despair and the headline writers had a field day with their puns. The *Sun* came over all Churchillian with their back-page headline which read, 'Never in the field of World Cup conflict has so little been offered by so few to so many.' The *Daily Mirror* had just one word for it: 'Aljeeria.' The *Guardian*, naturally, struck a more serious, ominous tone with: 'No spark, no spirit, no hope.' But in moments like this, when the public is venting its feelings, you need a bit of light relief, so my favourite was probably another *Mirror* headline: 'Booboozzzzzzelas.'

Unsurprisingly, Wayne Rooney apologised for his outburst at the end of the game. 'I am as passionate about the England team as anyone,' he said in a statement. 'Last night, on reflection, I said things in the heat of the moment that came out of frustration of both our performance and the result. For my part, I apologise for any offence caused by my actions at the end of the game. The most important thing now is to regroup, be positive and work towards winning the game on Wednesday. To do this the players will need the support of the fans more than ever.'

Too true. There probably isn't a fan in the whole of England who wants success more than the Manchester United striker, and he was understandably angry and frustrated with his own performance as well as England's. His reaction afterwards didn't offend me because it shows how much he cares. Far better that than traipse off the field with a contented smile on your face. England need to put this performance, well, in fact, these two performances, behind them and move on. It's also important for Rooney's reputation – and, let's not forget, he was forecast to be one of the big stars of this tournament – that he shows everyone he is the world-class player we think he is; in fact, we know he is. As much as I would like to say that England can do it without him, the truth is they can't. Our fate is inexorably linked to the form of our talisman. If England are to do exceptionally well at this tournament, they are going to need a fit and in-form Rooney.

Regular Rooney-watchers still question whether he has fully recovered yet from his ankle injury, but Capello flatly denies this and suggests that the problem is psychological. Asked outright if he was completely fit, Capello replied: 'Yes, completely fit. He's perfect. It's not a problem of this. The problem is in the mind.'

Rooney isn't the only one with a psychological problem, if that's what it is. The entire team seem to be suffering mentally. During the next five days, Capello and his staff need to work on restoring the players' self-belief. That and also take a long, hard look at his tactics. Whatever the formation, whether Gerrard plays behind Rooney or plays vaguely wide on the left, he must surely realise how unbalanced this team looks at present. If he does, he will perhaps then realise that their chronic inability to keep possession is related to the tactics.

There are rumours of dressing-room unrest and of the senior

players being unhappy with Capello's tactics, preparation and team selection. It makes me smile. It's always the same when a team are struggling at a World Cup. There may well be an element of that, but it's probably more a case of unrest in the press room than the dressing room. A World Cup is a long and expensive tournament, which means a lot of stories have to be written to justify a journalist's presence at them. They cannot write only about the matches.

Compared to the French, Capello's camp is all sweetness and light. Nicolas Anelka was sent home today for swearing at the coach, Raymond Domenech, during the interval in their 2–0 defeat to Mexico on Thursday, the French sports newspaper *L'Equipe* reported. Anelka was reported to have told Domenech to 'Go **** yourself, you son of a whore,' after Domenech had been critical of his tactical performance. Normally rows of that nature stay within the group, so clearly there has been a leak somewhere.

Without knowing the full facts, it's impossible to say with certainty who is to blame, although both Anelka and Domenech have form. Domenech has quarrelled with his players throughout the two years of qualifying and fell out with Florent Malouda, Anelka's Chelsea team-mate, only this week. As for Anelka, he's a long-time moody, as his omission from three consecutive World Cup squads would testify. With his talent, he should have comfortably made all three. It has to be said, though, since joining Chelsea a couple of years ago, there have been no reports of sulky behaviour, nor was there really at Arsenal.

Day nine saw the first country to be eliminated from these finals when Cameroon were beaten 2–1 by Denmark in Pretoria. This Cameroon side, although fun to watch, are not a patch on the one that shook the world in 1990 and gave the England side I played for a nasty surprise in the quarter-finals. They have been eliminated in the first round of every World Cup since then, except Germany '06 for which they failed to qualify. Despite 23 shots on goal, only once did anyone have the opportunity to dance with a corner flag à la Roger Milla and that was when Samuel Eto'o, restored to a central striking role, put them ahead. Arsenal's Nicklas Bendtner equalised before Dennis Rommedahl, the game's outstanding player, scored a sublime winner. Charlton fans must have been rubbing their eyes in disbelief, because I don't remember him looking this good in three seasons at the Valley.

Ghana's hopes are still alive, but up against ten men for three-quarters of their match against Australia in Rustenburg, they will have felt they should have done better than draw 1–1. It was the second consecutive match in which the Aussies have been reduced in numbers, but I didn't think Harry Kewell was as hard done-by as Tim Cahill had been in Australia's opening game against Germany. Pim Verbeek's side were a goal up through Brett Holman when a shot in the 25th minute from Jonathan Mensah struck the former Liverpool player – who was deputising for Cahill – on his arm as he stood by a post. Kewell protested vehemently and lengthily, but the replay was conclusive, even though Kewell kept pointing at it as though it was proof of his innocence. I thought Italian referee Roberto Rosetti made the right call, and FIFA confirmed the one-match ban. After struggling for so long to reach full fitness, it seems Kewell's efforts could be in vain. It's difficult to see Australia making the second round now. After that, Ghana let themselves down with their final ball.

At least we are now seeing teams trying to win matches rather than not lose them, even if the Netherlands remain disappointingly pragmatic. Whatever happened to Total Football? The great Rinus Michels would have turned in his grave watching the Dutch win ugly against Japan in Durban, and in so doing qualify for the second round. They have strength in depth, though, and Wesley Sneijder, one current Dutchman who would not have looked out of place in the 1974 team alongside Johan Cruyff, Johan Neeskens and Ruud Krol, scored the only goal of the game, a fierce drive which Eiji Kawashima could only parry into his own net. One quote from their manager, Bert van Marwijk, said all that one needed to know about his approach: 'I enjoyed watching Spain, but they lost one-nil. My sympathy is with Barcelona, but they lost the Champions League semi-final.'

Perhaps Brazil can restore his faith in football that is both winning and attractive. I can't wait for their match tomorrow against Ivory Coast, which we're covering live. Didier Drogba should give their impressive defence its first real test, assuming he is fully fit. Since fracturing his elbow he has been allowed to play with a lightweight cast, as I was, after some debate, in 1986, when I sprained my wrist quite badly. I can only assume his is a hairline fracture because there would be no way he could play so soon after a break. Mine was painful enough. Without the cast it would have been impossible.

Sunday 20 June

Slovakia 0 Paraguay 2
Italy 1 New Zealand 1
Brazil 3 Ivory Coast 1

There was mutiny in the air today at the World Cup, but unlike France, who refused to train, England's one was nipped in the bud before any serious harm could be done. John Terry, the former England captain, gave a press conference at Rustenburg, which started out innocently enough but ended up with what appeared to be a challenge to Capello's authority. Terry thought he was speaking on behalf of the players, but when he returned to the team hotel he quickly discovered he wasn't. Evidently, he had exceeded his authority when he suggested that a few home truths would be told at a team meeting this evening, adding 'if it upsets him [Capello] or any other player, so what?'

Most of the players were happy for Terry to talk in general terms about the team's shortcomings against Algeria, but they were less enamoured with his decision to get into specifics, like suggesting that only Rooney and Joe Cole – who has yet to play in this World Cup – were capable of unlocking defences. He also suggested that Capello might have to 'change his ways' and he joked that, like Anelka, 'maybe a few of us will be sent home this evening' after airing their views.

I can't believe the players were that unhappy with Terry, although Capello might have been. In the circumstances, I think the public needed a message from the team to prove that they cared and I thought Terry provided that, even if he did go a bit too far. If there was a frank and open discussion this evening between the players and the manager, it cannot have done any harm and might do a lot of good. I've heard all kinds of rumours about certain individuals behaving like prima donnas, but I'm sorry, I don't see Rooney demanding Perrier water in his bath. It's all symptomatic of a team that are struggling: player X is unhappy with player Y and they've got the hump with them; they're bored, they're fed up with baboons nicking food out of their rooms etc., etc. It will all disappear as if by magic with one decent win. Trust me.

Besides, I thought David Beckham was supposed to be the player liaison officer. I'm not sure what purpose he is serving there. I know he's on hand to assist with England's 2018 bid, but in terms of the performance of the team, he's obviously an irrelevance.

Although Terry denied that the players are consumed with fear, it was what I sensed in them when I sat in the Rustenburg stadium for an hour to watch England's match before heading back to the studio. There was a tension in the game that wasn't healthy; everyone seemed far too uptight. The players have got to enjoy it; they've got to make this their World Cup. They've got to tell themselves: 'This is what I've been waiting for all these years – let's show everyone what I'm made of.' It's up to Capello to instil those thoughts into his players. I used to love the big occasion, it's what it's all about. Sitting in the stadium watching them play, I got quite nervous. I'd much rather be out there on the pitch where you can influence matters – not that I could any more!

What the French did today may have got Fletcher Christian's support, but it wouldn't have got mine. Their refusal to train was inexcusable. However badly wronged Anelka may have been, the players had no right to take that sort of action. Even Zinedine Zidane, who has been critical of Domenech, lambasted them for their actions. Having claimed there was a 'traitor' in the camp who had leaked details of the bust-up to the press, Patrice Evra, the captain, became involved in an altercation with the team's fitness trainer, Robert Duverne, which ended with the latter storming off and hurling away his accreditation, in full view of the television cameras.

Once back on the bus, the players composed a statement that they insisted Domenech read out to the press. In it, they accused the French Football Federation of 'wilfully ignoring' Anelka's side of the story. Whereupon Jean-Louis Valentin, the team director, resigned in tears, declaring that he was 'sickened and disgusted' by the whole episode. With any luck, after tomorrow's game against South Africa, the rest of the France team will be following Anelka home. I suppose Laurent Blanc, who is set to succeed Domenech after this tournament, knows what he is letting himself in for.

The action had a lot to live up to, and Brazil did not disappoint, even if Ivory Coast did massively. It was a game that had everything: great goals, great skill and, not least, great controversy. If this one doesn't get them arguing down at the pub, nothing will. This was much more like watching Brazil. They're still clearly an uncharacteristically disciplined outfit, but no one could accuse them of lacking flair while they have players of the skill of Kaka, returning to something like his best form, Luis Fabiano and Robinho.

It was just a pity that referee Stephane Lannoy, in keeping with the performance of France's footballers at this World Cup, had a shocker. He got the big decisions hopelessly wrong. None more so than the one right at the end of the match when he sent off one of the world's greatest players, Kaka, and allowed the real villain of the piece, Ivory Coast's Kader Keita, to go completely unpunished. Keita had carelessly run into Kaka, catching the Brazilian's elbow in his chest. He went down holding his face.

Lannoy saw none of this; he was looking the other way at the time. And yet, after much prompting from Ivory Coast's players, he inexplicably arrived at the decision that he should show Kaka a second yellow card and with it a red while declining to punish Keita for the worst kind of cheating. Common sense would have told him that Kaka is not that kind of player. If FIFA do not rescind Kaka's red card and dish out a very heavy punishment to Keita they will be seen to be failing the game totally.

The other major talking point of the game, and Lannoy's first big mistake, was Luis Fabiano's second goal. It was a thing of beauty, but unfortunately he handled it not once but twice before muscling his way past Siaka Tiene and volleying it spectacularly home. Lannoy awarded the goal and then appeared to ask him whether he had handled it. We can guess his answer. It would be so easy to rid the game of this kind of skulduggery at World Cups, because the technology for resolving these issues is already in place. All that FIFA has to do is instruct referees to ask the player in question if he handled the ball. If he says he didn't and replays prove otherwise, he is handed an automatic two-match ban. Most players would own up, if they had any sense. Even Maradona might have come clean in 1986.

At least Fabiano's first-ever World Cup goal was legitimate, if slightly less impressive in its execution. Kaka, looking almost back to his best, set up the third for Elano, before Drogba punished a momentary lapse of concentration in the Brazilian defence with a header.

In all the excitement, New Zealand's historic 1–1 draw with the world champions Italy in Nelspruit was almost forgotten – and the Azzurri were lucky to get it! The Kiwis took the lead inside seven minutes with a goal from Shane Smeltz, which, it's probably fair to say, he never bargained for when he was playing for AFC Wimbledon, Mansfield and Halifax. The fact that it was a shade offside won't matter a jot to him. Italy were back level before the half-hour was up, when Daniele De Rossi needed just the slightest of shirt-tugs from Ipswich's Tommy Smith to fall flat on his face – momentarily *after* his shirt had been released. The New Zealanders claimed referee Carlos Batres had 'stars in his eyes' and he immediately awarded a penalty, which Vincenzo Iaquinta converted.

All these amazing results, great though they are for the World Cup's news value and for the underdog, are making me wonder more and more about whether the ball is playing a part in any of this. There are just too many mistakes at this World Cup. And the teams invariably on the wrong end of them are the Europeans, who play a different style to the South Americans, who are doing fine. I've played around with the ball and it's rubbish. Craig Johnston, the former Liverpool player who was on one of our programmes, prides himself on being a bit of an inventor and says the reason why it's useless is because it has eight panels whereas most balls have 32; as a result, it has less drag and is therefore more difficult to get up and over a defensive wall. Sounds reasonable.

Oh yes, and Paraguay virtually ensured their place in the second round by beating a very negative Slovakia side 2–0 with goals from Enrique Vera and Cristian Riveros.

Monday 21 June

Portugal 7 North Korea 0
Chile 1 Switzerland 0
Spain 2 Honduras 0

So, in the end, he kept his nerve and won. There must be a lesson there somewhere for England's footballers after Northern Ireland's Graeme McDowell held off the chasing pack to win the US Open, his first major, last night. I missed it. I forgot all about it after the exhausting day we had had. Alan Hansen hadn't. He stayed up until 3.30am watching it on television and when we met this morning he spent an hour and a half talking me through every shot. He loves his golf, Hansen, as we both do, and we know that Pebble Beach course rather well. We've been going there every year for about the last ten to play it. It's an annual thing. Hansen drifts between a 2 and a 3 handicap; I'm 5, but I haven't played much golf the last year or two, so I'm probably twice that figure at the moment. That and football is nearly all we ever talk about.

The news from the England camp today is that Terry has apologised to Capello for speaking out of turn, although he doesn't think he has been a disruptive influence in the camp. It's been suggested that the manager could discipline him by leaving him out of the match against Slovenia, but I would think that's most unlikely, if only because England are fast running out of centre-backs. Capello's comments on the matter seemed to confirm that. 'This is the big mistake, a very big mistake,' he said. 'But I hope that sometimes from the big mistake a big performance comes out.'

It obviously didn't go down well with him, having one of his players suggest who should play or who should not, in this case the promotion of Joe Cole. 'It's another mistake when you speak about one player, because there is no respect for the players that play before,' said Capello. 'Always the players think individually. I have to think about the team.'

The 'big mistake' will become a small one if England beat Slovenia on Wednesday. I don't see any of this internal 'strife' being much of an encouragement to the Slovenians – New Zealand's draw with Italy might be.

It was more like the real Spain in Johannesburg, where they

beat Honduras 2–0 with two excellent goals from David Villa, who must be among the favourites to win the Golden Boot here. He was a bit lucky to stay on the field, though, after shoving a hand in the face of Noel Valladares, the Honduras goalkeeper, who collapsed several seconds after contact was made. FIFA have got to stamp out this cheating. It's rife in the game now. It's the same with all the shirt-pulling at corners. If they started dishing out penalties it would stop overnight.

Fernando Torres still lacks a bit of sharpness since his injury at Liverpool. As Vicente Del Bosque, the Spain coach, remarked: 'Fernando is a great player. He knows – really knows – how to play on the limits of offside.'

I noticed that Torres also had some uncomplimentary things to say about the ball. 'We need to practise a bit more with this Jabulani because we are having a bit of bother with it,' he said. Nice to hear that we're not the only ones who think it's rubbish. And if Spain, with their excellent technique, are having problems with it, what chance the rest of us?

Poor North Korea suffered a bit of a reality check in their 7–0 defeat to Portugal – I bet they never showed that one on North Korean state television! The quality of Portugal's ball was just too good. Better still, Cristiano Ronaldo burst into life in the second half with a wonderfully selfless performance. Now all the great players of this tournament are up and running – except for Rooney. Incredibly, Portugal had six different names on the scorers' list – Raul Meireles, Simao, Hugo Almeida, Liedson, Ronaldo and two-goal Tiago.

Chile again impressed in their 1–0 defeat of Switzerland,

never mind that the Swiss had to play with ten men after the sending-off of Valon Behrami after half an hour. Torres may be struggling, but former Liverpool winger Mark Gonzalez was on target with a header. I just hope the South Americans maintain their penchant for attack.

Tuesday 22 June

Mexico 0 Uruguay 1
France 1 South Africa 2
Nigeria 2 South Korea 2
Greece 0 Argentina 2

Capello has made another exception to his policy of keeping the team selection to himself by informing Jermain Defoe this evening that he will start against Slovenia tomorrow in place of Emile Heskey. It's good news from the point of view of keeping the ball on the ground and goal scoring, but it does sound as though he is again going with 4–4–2, which is very disappointing. It hasn't happened for Defoe and Rooney as a pair so far, but that doesn't mean to say it can't work now. The word is that James Milner will replace Aaron Lennon on the right side of midfield, which at least should make us more robust in that area.

I was hoping – almost expecting – he would play Gerrard in a central role. It wouldn't be so bad if Gerrard stayed out on the left, but he doesn't; he naturally wanders in to a central position, leaving a nasty gap on that flank for opponents to exploit. I, like many other people, have my own theory about what sort of formation he should play and I offered it on our programme today. I think he should take a leaf out of Brazil's book – which is never a bad thing to do – and play with two holding players and leave the full-backs to provide the width. My line-up in a 4–2–3–1 formation would be: James; Johnson, Terry, Upson, A. Cole; Milner (or Carrick), Barry; Lampard, Gerrard, J. Cole; Rooney.

Although, as I have said before, whatever formation he sticks out there against Slovenia ought to be good enough to win. Capello is still thinking further ahead, which is encouraging to hear. 'I've got good players, but we're not at the top like we played in qualification,' he said. 'This group [of players] is really good, because I'm not crazy when I said my target is the final of the World Cup. I know this is a really good squad. I think not if, but when, we win, then all the teams have to fight against us. For me, it's a play-off, like a final in the Champions League, or a semi-final. That's the spirit we have to play. From the first moment we have to win.'

England have got to grasp this last chance they have of salvaging some pride, and in many ways the reputation of English football. If I were the England manager I would go around the team telling each and every one of them how great they are. Capello has to build up their confidence and remind them that they play in the strongest league in the world.

Concerns have been voiced over the choice of match officials for our game against Slovenia: we've got a German referee. But since Wolfgang Stark has refereed three of England's games before, all of which we have won, and he hasn't once issued a yellow card never mind a red one, I would suggest it bodes well for us.

Sadly, inevitably, the South African team bid farewell to this World Cup, but their spirit lives on in it. I'm so pleased they went out on a high, beating the ill-disciplined rabble from France 2–1. They may be the first host nation to be eliminated during the group stages, but that doesn't tell the whole story and it's worth emphasising that the four points they got would have been enough to get them through in some groups. We knew they were the weakest-ever home nation, but if anything they exceeded expectations and they can be very proud of a win over the former world champions, who reached the final last time – whatever the mental state of that side. It should have a good knock-on effect for the game here. It can leave a bit of a legacy. South Africa have been nothing if not refreshing.

In keeping with the rest of their World Cup campaign, France left sucking on sour grapes. In terms of public relations, it has been the worst I have ever witnessed. Domenech's refusal to shake hands afterwards with Carlos Alberto Parreira was unsporting and childish. As for turning his back on the great Brazilian manager, he should be utterly ashamed of himself, as should, I hope, the entire French nation. France leave South Africa with their heads not just bowed but between their knees.

Today was the 24th anniversary of Maradona's Hand of God goal, which means it was also the 24th anniversary of the greatest goal ever scored, and yet somehow the former has managed to upstage the latter. Who says good triumphs over evil? What most people don't realise is how great that second goal really was, when he dribbled the ball around Gary Stevens, Terry Butcher and finally Terry Fenwick before finishing it off quite beautifully. That pitch at the Azteca Stadium in Mexico City was one of the worst I have ever played on. It was newly laid in small sections of turf that moved as you ran on them. How he managed to score that goal on that pitch I will never ever know. When Maradona was playing, the pitch was never a great leveller.

The Argentina manager celebrated it by making Messi, the heir apparent to his throne, captain for the first time in the match against Greece, which was won 2–0 with goals from the two Martins, Demichelis and Palmero. At 23, he is the youngest to wear the armband at a World Cup finals. It was just a pity he couldn't crown it with his first goal of the tournament, but he did everything but score, despite being man-marked. He hit the post, had shots cleared off the goal-line and brought out the very best in goalkeeper Alexandros Tzorvas. Gentile himself would have been proud of the way Avraam Papadopoulos marked him. Of course, defence is the Greeks' byword. And yet Messi, unlike Maradona in similar circumstances, never once lost his cool. He is a star in every way. I would say he is in pole position to become the player of the tournament, followed by Ronaldo and Kaka, at the moment. Let's hope I'll be adding the name of Rooney before very long. Argentina enjoyed 82 per cent possession, the highest in a World Cup final match since 1966, when I wouldn't have thought they carried out such analysis.

On the subject of sportsmanship, it was good to see Uruguay and Mexico play out an honest game. They could have played for a draw, which would probably have put both teams through, but I suppose there was still a remote chance that South Africa or France could overtake the losers if they scored enough goals; the greater incentive though was to avoid facing Argentina in the round of 16. In the end, that privilege went to Mexico after losing 1–0 to a goal from Luis Suarez.

The 2–2 draw between Nigeria and South Korea will probably be best remembered for the worst miss in either mine or Alan Shearer's memory. Quite how Everton's Yakubu Ayegbeni managed it from three or four yards, I will never know. But at least he had the moral fortitude to step up and take a penalty a short while later, which he despatched quite perfectly. It's beginning to look as if we won't get an African nation through to the last 16. As I wrote earlier, I never thought any of them were candidates to become the first African winners of the World Cup, but I did think at least a couple of them would get through to the knockout stages. Ghana have looked the best organised. It's a pity they are missing their best player, Michael Essien. Similarly, it was a shame Drogba wasn't fully fit for Ivory Coast.

The BBC have had 8–10 million viewers for their evening games, and we've still got England to come! I cannot wait for tomorrow because that's when the World Cup really starts for us. The BBC have got every England game from then on. ITV got 17–19 million for their two England games, but because ours is in the afternoon, I don't think we'll get quite those sort of figures, but it should still be in the mid-teens. If we get through to the knockout stage, well, then it goes mad, you're talking 20-odd million.

I'm acutely aware of how big this is. I love the job. I get a real buzz from presenting – it's like scoring a goal, just different. My day usually starts at about ten, particularly in the first couple of weeks when we often have two games a day. I spend most of the morning talking to the editors about what we intend to put into the programmes other than the matches. Then I spend a couple of hours writing scripts, thinking about what questions to ask our guests, reviewing the hot topics of the day, and so on.

I also do quite a bit of homework on the teams who are playing that day. I usually go into the studio, without the resident pundits, about an hour before we go on air to rehearse one or two things. After that we get in a takeaway. Some days we do two shows back-to-back, but on those days when we have just an early game, I usually spend some time working on the following day's scripts. I invariably get back to the hotel quite late and go to bed shattered. It ends up being a long day and quite hard work, although I would hate for anyone to think I was complaining as I absolutely love doing it.

Wednesday 23 June

Slovenia 0 England 1
USA 1 Algeria 0
Ghana 0 Germany 1
Australia 2 Serbia 1

Big difference in performance. Tiny difference in result. England deservedly went through to the knockout stages here in Port Elizabeth by the only goal of the game against Slovenia, but they came within a hair's breadth of being eliminated – not to mention humiliated. Matthew Upson's instinctive, desperate last-ditch tackle on Tim Matavz in the penalty area in added-on time saved England's World Cup. Of course, it was always the plan for our second reserve central defender to come to the rescue here. Who needs Rio Ferdinand, Ledley King and Jamie Carragher?

The difference between staying on in a World Cup and possibly becoming heroes, even legends, and going home in disgrace is that fine. But it would have been a crime if England had not got through to the knockout stages, at least, because this was a display to erase from the memory completely the previous two apologies for a performance. I just hope the England players have erased them from theirs.

Even if Capello resisted the deafening calls to play Gerrard behind Rooney – not to mention recall Joe Cole to the starting line-up – this was a much better, balanced-looking formation, but more importantly England played far better individually, and with pace and tempo. As Upson said afterwards, 'We went about our job as if it was a Saturday afternoon in the Premier League – I think that's key for us.'

If England can carry on playing with this sort of tempo and spirit – which they can in these favourable weather conditions – they will cause many teams problems, starting, hopefully, with Germany. England were so close to navigating their way through the easier half of the draw. But, after the way we started this World Cup, we should be grateful that we are still in the competition.

Managers have to accept the brickbats as well as the bouquets, and on this occasion Capello deserved two dozen roses for selecting Defoe. To be fair, he invariably got it right during qualification, too. The Tottenham striker may not hold up the ball as well as Heskey, but he offers more options and is a far superior finisher, as he proved with his superbly taken goal in the 23rd minute, moving in front of Marko Suler to connect with one of numerous outstanding crosses from Milner. Defoe likes to get in behind defenders, which makes them worry about what's going on behind them as well as in front of them. That in turn makes more space for others, like Rooney. Heskey doesn't do that. He wins knockdowns.

Crucially, Gerrard gave a more disciplined performance, holding his position out on the left far better than he has done before here. The captain has probably been our best player, which hasn't always been the case when he pulls on an England shirt. Whether we can win playing old-style 4–4–2 against the better teams, I'm not sure. I still believe we need to flood the midfield more. Against the likes of Slovenia it was more than enough, and we should have won by two or three goals. We couldn't have asked for more to be playing the likes of Slovenia in a match we had to win.

The only negative was the sight of Rooney hobbling off with a recurrence of his ankle problem, but it didn't look serious and hopefully he will be fine for Sunday's match against Germany. He gave a much better account of himself while still not looking like the Rooney of earlier this year, the one who couldn't stop scoring, the one who was voted Player of the Year. Maybe that Rooney is just around the corner.

If Capello's tactics didn't change much, his personality seemed to undergo a complete transformation. I have never seen him that excited after a match. Marcel Desailly said he behaved in a manner that he never once saw in all their days together at Milan. When England achieved qualification against Croatia last September, he deliberately kept his distance from the celebrating players. Here, the cold, austere disciplinarian suddenly turned into a warm, passionate human being, shaking hands with the players – even Terry – before finally giving Gerrard a big hug. You could see how much it meant to him, how relieved he was. It's a huge burden to be carrying, the expectations of a nation – and it's not even his nation! As we all know, a winning camp is a happy camp. Afterwards, in a further moment of good humour, he declared that he had even allowed the players a beer the day before the game. Here's to you, Fabio.

We were so close to getting a second-round tie against the lesser G-force – Ghana. There was never much doubt that Germany would beat them later in the evening, which they duly did through a goal by Özil, but we prayed that Algeria would prove as awkward for the United States as they had been for us. For 92 minutes they were, although the Americans must have missed at least four sitters before Donovan secured victory deep into added-on time. The last-minute drama will have gone down well with American audiences – if they were watching. Actually, interest in the World Cup has picked up in the States and games like this might make them realise why the rest of the world loves football so.

Australia beating Serbia 2–1 makes you realise just how

global the game is nowadays, so it's about time the United States joined the party with greater gusto. It was good to see Cahill finish his World Cup on a high note with a goal after such an unfortunate start, but spare a thought for Serbia. The victors against Germany would surely have made the second round but for the refereeing of Uruguayan Jorge Larrionda, who disallowed two goals for offside and in the closing minutes turned down a penalty appeal. A goal by Holman proved to be the winner after Marko Pantelic finished up with a late goal for Serbia that was anything but a consolation. The good news was that it meant at least one African nation goes through to the next round.

What with French President Sarkozy meeting up with Thierry Henry to discuss France's debacle and the Italian Federal Reforms Minister, Umberto Bossi, having to retract his claim that Italy would 'buy' a victory against Slovakia tomorrow to ensure qualification for the next round, this World Cup is getting pretty serious. As the great Bill Shankly said, 'Football's not a matter of life and death – it's more important than that'.

Venue:	Nelson Mandela Bay Stadium, Port Elizabeth
Attendance:	36,893
England:	James; Johnson, Terry, Upson, A. Cole; Milner, Barry, Lampard, Gerrard; Defoe (Heskey 86), Rooney (J. Cole 72)
Scorer:	Defoe (23)
Yellow card:	Johnson (48)
Slovenia:	Handanovic; Brecko, Suler, Cesar, Jokic; Birsa, Koren, Radosavljevic, Kirm (Matavz 79); Ljubijankic (Dedic 62), Novakovic
Yellow card:	Jokic (40), Birsa (79), Dedic (81)
Shots:	England 8/13, Slovenia 6/13
Possession:	England 54%, Slovenia 46%
Referee:	Wolfgang Stark (Germany)

10

Expectation; elimination; humiliation

Slovakia 3 Italy 2

Paraguay 0 New Zealand 0

Denmark 1 Japan 3

Cameroon 1 Netherlands 2

The British redtops, searching desperately for lucky omens, were putting great stock by the fact that England were matching the class of '90 game for game, scoreline for scoreline, which meant that this England just *had* to reach the semi-finals – like the England team I played for. I hope they are right; indeed, I hope they can go at least one better. The big difference is that we played Belgium in the second round, albeit a very good Belgian side, while this England team have got our old nemesis – Germany. 'No problem,' said our confident media. Under a front-page headline 'Germans Wurst at Penalties', the *Sun* produced statistics that showed that over a four-year period the current England players have been more successful than their German counterparts at converting penalties and that David James, our goalkeeper, has a better record of saving them than his opposite number, Manuel Neuer.

All good, harmless fun, I suppose, and maybe good for our morale, too – who knows? Whether or not it's penalties again, there's certainly a good chance of it going to extra time, since all four meetings between the two countries at the knockout stage in major competitions have done: World Cup '66, '70 and '90, and Euro 96, the last two ending famously in penalty shoot-outs, which, as everyone knows, we lost. And, since there's not much to choose between the two teams this time, there must be a very good chance of another dramatic finale, hopefully with a different outcome. Having converted 16 out of 17 penalties at World Cups, Germany obviously have a good record, but none of that will count for anything when the moment comes – if it comes. Nor will the fact that of the 27 times we've met, we lead 12–10 – if you discount penalty shoot-outs. All I will say is that there is only one team out of the two who have missed a penalty at this World Cup, and it is not England.

The English media were also grabbing at every crumb of comfort they could find and seizing upon any perceived slights, such as Franz Beckenbauer's unwise remark that England were 'stupid' to end up finishing second in their group. The reason he said that was that Bobby Charlton's old adversary had wanted to see England and Germany meet at a more fitting stage of the competition, rather than in the second round, but such respect for the old rivalry was conveniently lost in the 'slanderous' attack on England's good name. Having said that, Jürgen Klinsmann tells me that Beckenbauer is apt to speak out of turn at times and say strange things.

While Beckenbauer was busy doing Capello's pre-match motivational speech for him, Joachim Löw, the Germany coach, tried to redress matters, and in the process perhaps soften up England, by describing them as a 'wonderful team' who have not shown their best form so far. 'This England team will be incredibly dangerous for us,' he said, and he has warned his players that Wayne Rooney 'is always ready to explode'. By that, I hope he means his form rather than his temperament.

Klinsmann rather enjoys the self-deprecating humour of the British media and wishes the German media didn't take themselves quite so seriously all the time. I told him it's because we're so used to failure. The main trouble with our media is that they view England either as useless or we're the best in the world. So, after beating the smallest nation at this World Cup, we're now the greatest. One of these days they're going to be right.

It would appear Fabio Capello is looking for portents, too, and has insisted that we play in red again – someone must have told him we did rather well in that colour once before, other than against Slovenia. The England coach has told his players that if it does come to penalties they should pick their spot and stick to it, which is good advice. It's what I always did and I discovered the other day, while chatting to Alan Shearer, it's what he always did. Once chosen, like me, he would practise the same penalty over and over again in training. Indecision at the last moment can be fatal. Sometimes you have to change your tactic, when you get awarded a second penalty, as we did against Cameroon in 1990. I decided that since the goalkeeper had dived early and the wrong way for the first one, I would hit the second one down the middle, which I did, and, fortunately, it went in.

People were joking that Stuart Pearce would get involved in the penalty coaching. Pearce may have missed that one in 1990, but he was a great penalty-taker because he was such a good striker of the ball, as he aptly demonstrated in the penalty shoot-out against Spain at Euro 96. The sight of Psycho courageously stepping up to take responsibility and banishing his demons will remain for me one of the great moments of England football history. I bet Chris Waddle and Gareth Southgate would love to have had the opportunity to do likewise in a major tournament. The fact is we have all missed penalties, those who are good at taking them and those who are not so good.

It's very much a case of how you feel on the day as to whether you volunteer, so it's difficult to say who should take them if there is a shoot-out. Besides, you don't know who will still be on the pitch. Frank Lampard, as our nominated penalty-taker, will obviously take one; so, too, will Wayne Rooney, if he is fit. Other candidates would be Steven Gerrard, James Milner and Jermain Defoe, although I understand Gerrard fretted for months before the last World Cup about taking one and when it eventually came to it he failed, so perhaps the skipper will be one of those who decline this time. I think we've got a good bunch of penalty-takers. But we've got two hours of football before then, so perhaps we should worry about it if and when it happens.

This match is going to bring back a lot of memories for me. People often ask me if I have any regrets and I always tell them I have absolutely none. Disappointment? Yes – massive. It is the one moment of my career when I look back and think: 'If only . . .' If only Andy Brehme's free-kick hadn't deflected off Paul Parker and looped fortuitously over Peter Shilton in goal; if only we had been awarded a penalty when Chris Waddle was brought down; if only Waddle's shot had been a couple of inches the other way, it might have hit the back of the net instead of the post; if only Pearce's kick in the shoot-out hadn't struck one of Bodo Illgner's legs; if only Waddle hadn't skied his penalty kick. It's all ifs and maybes, I know, but I remain convinced we would have beaten Argentina in the final. This is a second-round match not a semi-final, so there's not so much at stake, but it's still a game we have to win if we want to claim the ultimate prize. England don't want any regrets or disappointments.

We're expecting a huge television audience on Sunday. The fine weather in England is expected to continue until then, so that might affect the audience figures, but I can't believe many people would rather sit in the sun than go through the excruci-ating agony of watching England play! I'm expecting an audience of well over 20 million. We've got an hour to fill before kick-off, so this morning we've been going through possible preview material and it's hard to know what to leave out rather than what to put in. There's been so much history over the years between England and Germany: '66, '70, '90, '96, Shearer's winner against them at Euro 2000; the 5–1 win against them in Munich in 2001 – so many memories, but we could do with adding another happy one.

This World Cup of shocks got another one today, although so poor have Italy been here that they probably had the tomatoes at the ready at Fiumicino Airport prior to the world champions' defeat to Slovakia. They may not be departing the tournament quite as shambolically as France, the runners-up four years ago, did two days ago, but it has, nevertheless, been an uncharacteristically chastening experience for the four-time winners, who failed to win a single match and, as a result, for the first time in their history, finished bottom of their group. Even more uncharacteristic was their defending against the Slovaks, which was a shambles. This was the first time the two finalists from the previous World Cup have been eliminated at the group stage.

They had been in a group that the Italy of old would have walked. It's proved to be a tournament too far for a lot of their players. Paradoxically, the dearth of Italian talent had been highlighted by the Champions League final, which, though won by Inter Milan, did not contain a single Italian in the starting line-up. Marcello Lippi, Italy's veteran coach, cut an honourable figure in defeat – unlike Domenech – accepting full responsibility for his team's failure. He will be replaced by Cesare Prandelli. 'I evidently was not able to prepare them as I had

John Terry speaks his mind at a press conference in the aftermath of the Algeria game. His call for Joe Cole to be given a more prominent role did not go down well with the manager.

Jermain Defoe rewarded Fabio Capello for putting him in the starting line-up with a great poacher's goal from James Milner's excellent cross from the right wing. This was what we had all been waiting for.

Matthew Upson became John Terry's third starting partner at centre-back in the tournament, and helped secure a win with this late, crucial tackle on Tim Matavz.

It wasn't the only time England's defence required desperate measures, as John Terry and Glen Johnson combine to block the way to goal.

Fabio Capello joins his team on the pitch to celebrate qualification through to the round of 16. England had improved, but now things were getting serious as an old foe awaited them: Germany.

The manager lays down the law in training before the game against Germany, but there is still time for some fun.

Lukas Podolski scores Germany's second, after more poor England defending.

Matthew Upson's towering header pulled a goal back for England, raising brief hopes of a comeback.

Manuel Neuer looks behind him to see the ball had crossed the line after Frank Lampard's great strike which would have brought the scores level. Unfortunately, none of the officials was sure and the goal did not count.

Thomas Müller celebrates scoring Germany's fourth goal to confirm England's worst-ever defeat in the World Cup finals. The sad truth was that it could have been even worse.

England captain Steven Gerrard knows it's all over for another four years.

Fabio Capello faces the press after England's disappointing tournament, but could provide few answers. While Frank Lampard knows that England were a long way short of finding any glory in South Africa.

Diego Forlan scores Uruguay's equaliser in the semi-final against the Netherlands. His excellent performances earned him the FIFA Golden Ball as the best player in the tournament.

Three minutes into the quarter-final, and Golden Boot winner Thomas Müller scores past Sergio Romero to set Germany on their way to a 4–0 victory over Argentina. At least England scored against them.

After being on the receiving end of many fouls, the brilliant Andres Iniesta scores the winning goal late in extra time to give Spain a deserved 1–0 victory over the Netherlands in the World Cup final.

Iker Casillas lifts the Jules Rimet trophy as Spain celebrate becoming world champions for the first time in their history. Few would begrudge them the title, as they played beautiful football.

hoped,' he said. 'If a team plays poorly, as we did for seventy-five minutes, there can be only one culprit: the manager. I thought we were ready – clearly we were not.'

If nothing else, the Italians played their part in a thrilling conclusion to the match, as they struggled to get back on terms after falling behind to two goals from Robert Vittek. Antonio Di Natale halved the deficit with a tap-in and, although Kamil Kopunek restored the Slovaks' two-goal advantage, Fabio Quagliarella immediately hit back for Italy with a delightful chip in added-on time. With the other game in the group between Paraguay and New Zealand still goalless, Italy knew a draw would send them through and, right at the death, they seemed to have got it when a golden opportunity presented itself to Simone Pepe at the far post, but the Udinese midfielder some-how contrived to miss it. The match, which contained one or two controversial incidents, was very capably refereed by England's Howard Webb. He may prove to be England's best performer here.

'I haven't seen the replays, but I thought he did a solid job,' said Italy's Andrea Pirlo. 'But in any case, the referee had noth-ing to do with our exit. We were not good enough. It's not just his [Lippi's] fault, it's our fault, too. We could have done better and should have done better, but when you go home without winning a single game in a group like this one, you just have to look at yourself. Our performance was shameful.'

The most impressive performance of all, I thought, belonged to Japan. It was obvious from England's friendly against them before the World Cup, which England were fortunate to win with two own goals, that they were a very capable side. I spent a year in Japan at the end of my career, which unfortunately was marred by a toe injury, but I thoroughly enjoyed my time there and it was good to see how much they have progressed, even since their own World Cup finals in 2002. They are well organised and good going forwards.

But it was to the surprise of most people that they beat Denmark, and quite comfortably, too. The 3–1 win was embellished by a couple of excellent free-kicks from Keisuke Honda and Yasuhito Endo, and we haven't seen too many of those in this competition. Honda actually managed to get his up and over a wall, which has proved almost impossible for some of the more celebrated dead-ball experts, while Endo bent his around the wall.

There may have been more than a hint of culpability from goalkeeper Thomas Sorensen, but they were both great strikes. Prior to this, only two players at this World Cup had scored from free-kicks – Kalu Uche of Nigeria and Park Chu Young of South Korea. Jon Dahl Tomasson, in what is likely to be his final game for Denmark, was fortunate to get a second chance after fluffing his spot-kick, but Japan deservedly had the final word with a goal from Shinji Okazaki.

It meant that Japan qualified for the round of 16, thereby equalling their 2002 best performance. They now face Paraguay. Not far behind them among the long shots who beat the big shots were New Zealand, who with three points finished above the world champions Italy in Group F. If they had scored one more goal in any of their games they would have won the group – that's how close they came to making history and how close these groups can be. Anyway, they have already made plenty here by going three games unbeaten. At their only previous appearance in the finals, in 1982, they lost all three.

Even so, it made you question whether we are witnessing a narrowing of the gap between the game's established countries and the emerging ones, or whether this World Cup, with its plastic beach ball, is just throwing up a lot of freak results. Whatever it is that's happening, the football in the last few days has been a lot more fun to watch. Understandably, there was little doubt in the mind of Ricki Herbert, the New Zealand coach, about the authenticity of the results, at least in his team's case, and he actually left the tournament disappointed. 'A lot of people thought because we had amateurs we weren't good enough,' he said. 'That's dead and buried now.'

The Netherlands made it three wins in three games in Group E, but it wasn't good enough for their coach, Bert van Marwijk, who described their 2–1 win against Cameroon as 'sloppy' and insisted that his team must do better against Slovakia in the round of 16. A little surprisingly, with qualification already guaranteed, he chose to field a couple of players who were on yellow cards. He probably wanted to ensure they faced Slovakia rather than Paraguay, and also maintain their momentum. Robin van Persie, sorely in need of competitive action after so long out through injury, was given an hour and the Arsenal player responded with a fine opening goal. After Samuel Eto'o equalised from the penalty spot, van Marwijk decided to give another of his recovering stars a 20-minute run-out, and again the response was good. With seven minutes remaining, Arjen Robben danced inside Rigobert Song to hit the post with a cracking drive, from which Klaas-Jan Huntelaar followed up to score. Song goes out on a high note, having become the first African to appear in four World Cups.

My wife Danielle and her little girl Ella came out a few days ago. We took her to a cheetah reserve. Because the BBC have got both England's game and Argentina's on Sunday, I've got the day off on Saturday – my first – so we propose to go on a safari a few hours' drive from Cape Town with my son Harry and his girl-friend, who have just arrived.

Friday 25 June

Portugal 0 Brazil 0
North Korea 0 Ivory Coast 3
Chile 1 Spain 2
Switzerland 0 Honduras 0

We had wondered whether Spain might become the third major power to depart this tournament prematurely. We should not have doubted them, although we did during the opening twenty minutes or so, when Chile more than lived up to their new-found reputation. Unfortunately, the South Americans are seriously flawed temperamentally. Their over-exuberant tackling was bound to get them into trouble, and it eventually did when the excellent Marco Estrada picked up a second yellow, even if Fernando Torres went down all too easily. The Liverpool striker may be suffering with his form and fitness, but, fortunately for Spain, David Villa is not. So when a moment of madness from Chile goalkeeper Claudio Bravo presented him with the ball and an open goal, he happily accepted it, even though he was 40 yards from goal at the time. Even so, Spain need a fit Torres almost as badly as we need a fit Wayne Rooney – in their case to win the tournament, in ours to acquit ourselves properly.

Before half time, Andres Iniesta had made certain of victory, although a goal early in the second half from Chile's Rodrigo Millar meant that Spain could not relax until the closing stages, when it became clear that Switzerland, who needed a two-goal win against Honduras, were labouring towards a goalless draw. Spain, whose priority had been to avoid a round of 16 match with Brazil, spent the last few minutes playing the ball along their back line, while Chile, who were now happy just to qualify, dutifully sat off. It was not a particularly edifying sight, but an inevitable one. The good news is that Spain now come here to Cape Town to face Portugal and we're covering that game. The winners of it are looking very good to reach the final.

'I think we've overcome a very difficult time,' Vicente Del Bosque, the Spain coach, said. 'We were very disturbed emotionally by the defeat to Switzerland, but we are more optimistic now and I'm sure that will be reflected on the pitch.'

After the Lord Mayor's Show it might have been, but thank goodness it was, because the main feature of the day (Brazil versus Portugal) was a bitter disappointment. It all became far too personal, and both sides seemed to lose sight of their objective – although perhaps they didn't, because a draw was always likely to be enough to send both teams through to the knockout stages. In short, it was nothing like the spectacle that a crowd of 62,712 – the first match other than those involving the host nation to become a sell-out – can have hoped for. Seven yellow cards, all before half time – four to Portugal, three to Brazil – told its own story. Without the unfairly suspended Kaka, the injured Elano and Robinho rested, Brazil were never likely to be at their best.

Ivory Coast's World Cup ended with a respectable 3–0 win against North Korea, thanks to goals from Yaya Toure, Romaric and Salomon Kalou, and Sven-Goran Eriksson, their coach, telling them 'they should be very proud of themselves and the country should be proud of them'. The question is: was England's former manager proud of himself or to be specific his tactics, notably in Ivory Coast's crucial opening game against Portugal, which finished in a goalless draw? Some would say he held this free-spirited side back when their only hope of qualifying from this very awkward group was to be bold. Once Portugal had run riot against North Korea, their World Cup dreams were over. So, too, now is Eriksson's tenure as manager. Apparently, he has not ruled out a return to English football.

Uruguay 2 South Korea 1
United States 1 Ghana 2 (aet)

Our safari – which included a 5a.m. start – was disappointingly tame, more like a trip to Longleat than the African jungle; so much for seeing wild animals in their natural environment. I understand the German team went on a similar trip yesterday and that, with careful cropping at London newspaper picture desks, it has produced some interesting images: in short, Germans looking terrified of three lions. We shall see whether that proves to be the case.

I'm past predicting the outcome of matches at this World Cup. A classic? I've no idea. All I can say for sure is that the expectation will be incredible, that there will be drama and nerve-wracking excitement. Sport is at its finest when it's at its most excruciating. I just hope we finally see the best of Rooney, because I think if we do we will win. I suppose we might as well get our excuses in early. The English season is very demanding physically, there's no doubt about that.

I remember Peter Beardsley and John Barnes looking jaded at Euro 88 after a particularly long, hard season with Liverpool, so it can leave its mark on a player. Personally, I sometimes struggled the season after a major championship. When championships finish, you are pretty much straight back into training for the new season. If you have had a good championship, the euphoria keeps you going for a while and then

189

mid-season, about Christmas time in my case, you run out of steam. But you're better off feeling tired and lethargic in January than you are in June/July in a championship year. I remember that happening to me a couple of times.

If you survive long enough in the tournament, you can sometimes get your form back. It must have something to do with bio-rhythms, but at Italia '90 we didn't know about such things then. All I know is I felt okay for the first game against the Republic of Ireland and then out of sorts for the matches against the Netherlands and Egypt. In the second round, against Belgium, I got some zip back into my game, and in the quarters and semis I was flying.

A lot of Rooney's game is about commitment and brute strength and, allied to the injuries he picked up towards the end of the season, it's perhaps no surprise he has looked a bit lacklustre here. None of us, probably, has ever seen him play as he did against Algeria when even simple ball control deserted him. Some people outside the game wonder how a great player can look so inept. But it can happen. I suppose it's the equivalent of the yips in golf. I understand Lukas Dlouhy, the Czech Republic tennis player, served 27 double faults in a doubles match at Wimbledon yesterday. You might ask, 'How can that happen, he's a Grand Slam champion?' But the fact is it can and it does.

I know exactly what will be going through Rooney's mind right now. He'll be wondering, 'How will I feel on Sunday?' I don't think he doubts his ability for a moment. It's that fickle thing called form. It often comes from a bad start, and then confidence wanes and you get edgy and tight. He's got to try to relax and enjoy it, but it's easier said than done. Some people wonder how on earth can he play on his own up front, as many people like myself believe, when he is in such poor shape, but actually it's physically easier. When he plays in that position off a main striker, he invariably goes hunting the ball in deep positions and ends up working twice as hard. If he was played up front in the right system, he would get plenty of support from Steven Gerrard and Frank Lampard.

If we're going to play two out-and-out strikers tomorrow, we will need to be very narrow in midfield or they will play through us. Gerrard has to put the team before himself and be disciplined and stay wide on the left to keep our shape. The trouble is, he's such an instinctive player, and if he's not getting involved he will naturally roam infield. That's the main problem with this 4–4–2 system that Capello plays. We saw that in England's second game. This is not a great German side, by their standards, and certainly not a patch on the one at Italia '90. For one thing, it's much younger. I prefer Germany's system, but I prefer our players and ultimately players should always triumph over systems – shouldn't they? Apparently, their midfielder Bastian Schweinsteiger has a hamstring problem. He's an essential part of their system, so if he's unfit that could cause some disruption to the way they play. I think it's fifty-fifty.

I'm pleased Ghana won today, because now we have an African presence in the quarter-finals. All of Africa is getting behind them. They have been the best of that continent's six teams and, after beating the United States, this young side could become the first African country to make the semi-finals of a

World Cup. The States, watched by former president Bill Clinton, were gritty and resilient to the last. Bouncing back from an early goal by Portsmouth's Kevin-Prince Boateng – who seems to have put the disappointment of missing a penalty in the FA Cup final behind him – they took the game into extra time thanks to a penalty from Landon Donovan. Inevitably, Asamoah Gyan, with his third goal of the tournament, won it with a volley.

It's just a pity they will be without the midfielder Andre Ayew, who is now suspended, for what is a fairly even-looking quarter-final against Uruguay. Two goals from Luis Suarez – the second a beautifully executed, not to mention timely, shot that went in off a post – were enough to dash South Korea's hopes after Lee Chung-Yong's equaliser and send the South Americans into their first quarter-final in forty years.

Sunday 27 June

Germany 4 England 1
Argentina 3 Mexico 1

And we worried about a penalty shoot-out? We should have been so lucky. If such ways of deciding a football match unfairly make a scapegoat of somebody, how just that on this occasion defeat to Germany in regulation time made a scapegoat of eleven individuals and a couple of substitutes – oh, yes, and a linesman.

It was obvious from as early as the fifth minute, when Mesut Özil got behind Ashley Cole and drew a tricky save from David

James with his legs, that a penalty shoot-out was not going to be required to separate the two sides this time. Luck would not come into it. In fact, it did when Frank Lampard was denied a perfectly good goal in the 38th minute, because a well-positioned linesman could not see that the ball had crossed the goal-line by all of two feet, but it had little bearing on the outcome of this match. Germany could have given England a two-goal start and still beaten them, so superior were they.

That's why it was so absurd that England should give them all the help they could. It beggared belief that players playing in arguably the most important match of their lives could play so poorly. Worse still, play so naively. To describe three of the four goals as schoolboy errors would be disrespectful to schoolboy football, which I don't remember ever being quite as bad as this. Without question the mistakes were down to gross individual errors by top Premier League players, but, that said, their manager hardly gave them a helping hand.

Fabio Capello has won more major league titles than any man has a right to, as well as a memorable Champions League final, so how can he possibly put out a team that was so unbalanced, so disjointed, so dysfunctional? They looked like a team that had been thrown together with zero preparation. While the England manager's job may well be cursed, it surely can't turn a wise man into a fool – or can it?

After a defeat like this, it would be easy to say that English players just aren't good enough, aren't anywhere near as great as the hype builds them up to be, and there is a semblance of truth in that. But the England players on show in Bloemfontein, Cape

Town and Rustenburg, for all their faults, don't normally play like this. Something has gone terribly awry with them since they qualified in style last September.

From the very start of this World Cup, they have played like a team consumed with the fear of failure. Perhaps they have been guilty of believing some of their own publicity. Somebody needed to tell them right at the start of this competition: 'Don't worry, you're not the favourites – nothing like.' Perhaps then they might have relaxed and played a bit more like they normally do in a league which, after all, is more pressurised than most.

I've never felt England were good enough to win this competition, but I did think, at full strength, we were good enough to give a decent account of ourselves. Of course, we haven't been at full strength, but even a weakened England team, properly organised, should have travelled further in the competition than this. It wasn't a case of being unlucky and drawing Germany. Even if we had won our group, I don't believe we would have beaten Ghana on this form.

The win against Slovenia had raised our hopes – that was all. We should have known better than to think – to hope – we had turned the corner. It's not as if Germany exposed chinks in our defensive armour. We already knew they were there – notably the lack of pace – but we should have protected them better, which Capello's old-fashioned 4–4–2 comprehensively failed to do. The extraordinary thing was that, like everyone else, he must have seen it, but did nothing about it. For example, we knew well in advance that if given the opportunity, the wonderful Özil would lead us a merry dance in that space between our back four and midfield. Yet little or no effort was made to restrict his movement, although, to be fair, the one-paced Gareth Barry couldn't get near him.

Pace, time and again, was an issue, never more so than with Germany's first goal. It may have been largely down to dreadful positioning by John Terry and Matthew Upson, but one couldn't help feel that Rio Ferdinand would have got back at Miroslav Klose and snuffed out the danger. To concede a goal straight from a goal-kick at this level of the game is unbelievable. Perhaps we need Wimbledon back in the Premier League to sharpen up the minds of our centre-backs. It was part of Joachim Löw's plan to draw Terry and Upson out of position, but even he must have been taken aback at how willingly they obliged in that moment. It was Klose's fiftieth international goal – I'll never catch him now.

England's response was a header from Jermain Defoe, which hit the bar, but they weren't even allowed to take some pride in that because the linesman wrongly adjudged him to be offside. Germany, on the other hand, left nothing to chance as the ball was moved briskly from Özil to Klose to Thomas Müller and finally to Lukas Podolski, and the Cologne player's unerring left foot did the rest.

I'm not sure anyone could see an England goal coming, but come one did when Steven Gerrard crossed for Upson, hanging splendidly in the air as if by an invisible cable, to send a thumping header past Manuel Neuer in goal. It is amazing what a goal can do for a team, and England were suddenly energised by it. Within a minute, Lampard, momentarily looking like that other fellow at Stamford Bridge who scores twenty goals a season from midfield, drove a shot of just the right pace over the head of Neuer and against the bar. The ball came down clearly over the line – without any need for anyone to see it again in slow motion – and Capello leaped from his seat to celebrate. But the Uruguayan referee Jorge Larrionda was possibly unsighted and his assistant Mauricio Espinosa, who certainly wasn't, suddenly suffered myopia. No goal. The use of goal-line technology is a no-brainer as far as I'm concerned, but, as I say, on this occasion you shouldn't have even needed it.

Was this going to be how we lost to the Germans this time, by a diabolical refereeing decision? No, thank goodness. It didn't stop the automatic response from some in such a situation, which is: 'You go in at half time at two-two instead of two-one, and all of a sudden it's a different game.' Well, it might have been, but I think probably not. What I do know is that England would have been the luckiest team on the planet to be level at half time. Unfortunately, what it did do was make them lose their heads in the second half and become ridiculously gung-ho. England were trailing 2–1 not 4–1 (that was still to come), and yet they were piling forwards like it was the last five minutes of the game instead of the last 25.

A poor first touch from Barry close to the opposition's penalty area was all it took for these eager young German beavers to take advantage and, before you could say Bastian Schweinsteiger – nothing much wrong with his hamstring – the ball was whisked upfield, as England players gave chase as if with lead in their boots. Schweinsteiger left the 'fleet-footed' Johnson for dead before despatching the ball to Müller, whose finish from fifteen yards is becoming a given at this World Cup.

If Germany had any compassion for their old enemy, they would have left it at that. After all, the point had been pretty emphatically made. But no such luck. Özil chose instead to embarrass Barry one more time, before skipping away down the left wing to cut inside and give Müller another chance to show James no mercy.

After that, all an Englishman needed to see was Diego Maradona raising his hand in triumph as Argentina benefited from another refereeing gaffe. It was like Mexico '86 all over again. Mind you, judging by the way they despatched Mexico in 2010, Germany may have saved us from an even greater humiliation. Rather them than us facing this attacking fury in Cape Town next Saturday. Thanks to the beauty of technology – even if we don't fully use it – we were able to see that Carlos Tevez was two yards offside when he gave Argentina the lead. We needed a slow-motion camera to catch the Manchester City striker's second, which must have been the hardest shot of this World Cup. By then Gonzalo Higuain had already doubled their advantage with a cheap goal. Mexico's consolation was a goal from Manchester United's recent acquisition, Javier Hernandez, which meant that the red half of Manchester also had something to cheer about. But what about the rest of us?

Venue: Free State Stadium, Mangaung, Bloemfontein

Attendance: 40,510

England: James; Johnson (Wright-Phillips 87), Terry, Upson, A. Cole; Milner (J. Cole 64), Barry, Lampard, Gerrard; Defoe (Heskey 71), Rooney

Scorer: Upson (37)

Yellow card: Johnson (81)

Germany: Neuer; Lahm, Friedrich, Mertesacker, Boateng; Schweinsteiger, Khedira; Müller (Trochowski 72), Özil (Kiessling 83), Podolski; Klose (Gomez 72)

Scorers: Klose (20), Podolski (32), Müller (67, 70)

Yellow card: Friedrich (47)

Shots: England 9/19, Germany 7/17

Possession: England 51%, Germany 49%

Referee: Jorge Larrionda (Uruguay)

11

European champions, world champions

Monday 28 June

Netherlands 2 Slovakia 1
Brazil 3 Chile 0

While Fabio Capello laid the blame for England's defeat to Germany squarely on the 'incredible' decision to disallow Frank Lampard's goal, most of us could see reasons for it that left nothing to chance. England were comprehensively beaten by a team who had most things on their side: better technique, greater talent (on this evidence), a youthful zest and, not least, vastly superior tactics.

Compared to the treatment some of his predecessors received

199

at the hands of the media, the England manager seemed to get off quite lightly. In fact, the *Daily Mail* seemed to be in two minds about whether he should stay or go. 'A man of honour would resign, Capello,' said one headline in that newspaper, while another read: 'England need Fabio now more than ever'.

Inevitably, he was asked if he would resign and equally inevitably he replied: 'Absolutely not!' He said he would seek talks with Club England chairman, Sir Dave Richards, to discuss his future. 'I need to know whether the FA have confidence in me or not,' he said. The cost to the FA, should they decide to sack him and his backroom staff, now that the get-out clause in his contract has been removed, is estimated to be about £12 million, which is a very good reason for not sacking him.

Interestingly, Frank Lampard, the scorer of the goal that wasn't, said he wanted Capello to stay on. The Chelsea midfielder's view has to be respected, but I'm not sure that his after-match view of how the game went should be. 'Nobody can stand here and tell me Germany were a lot better than us,' he said. 'They were not four-one better than us.' Oh yes they were.

His Chelsea team-mate – for a short while longer, anyway – Joe Cole showed rather greater perception with his comment that England 'weren't good enough from the start of the friendlies'. Another remark he made, that there were a 'lot of issues', was seized upon by the media who saw it as a thinly veiled criticism of camp life with Capello. It remains to be seen whether such inferences are justified.

In the main, the media went for general criticism of the team, which was probably about right. 'Muellered', said the *Sun*;

'Torn to Fritz', said the *Daily Mirror*; 'Old guard reveal all old failings', said *The Times*. Whichever way you looked at it, it made for uncomfortable reading for our national team and their supporters.

Germany, on the other hand, rejoiced in the irony that they had got their own back for that critical Geoff Hurst goal against them in the 1966 final when a Russian linesman, arguably less well positioned than this Uruguayan one, decided that the West Ham striker's shot against the crossbar had indeed bounced over the line. Coincidentally, the player on this occasion was also a product of the famous West Ham academy. You couldn't write it. It didn't stop German Chancellor Angela Merkel apologising to Prime Minister David Cameron as they watched the game together at the G20 summit in Toronto, Canada.

The image of Rooney intimating with his hands to Mauricio Espinosa by how much the ball had crossed the line, as the players left the field at half time, and the Uruguayan linesman's dismissive response was still painfully fresh in the mind. It helped only a smidgeon to learn that back in Uruguay referee Jorge Larrionda's decision to disallow the goal was described as 'the error which stained a career', and that when shown a replay of the incident he groaned, 'Oh my God,' which is definitely an improvement on 'Hand of God'.

The defeat gave Franz Beckenbauer the opportunity to stick the boot into his old rivals one more time. 'England were overwhelmed,' said the former World Cup-winning captain. 'They just could not come to terms with our style of play. We have taken England apart.'

There wasn't that feeling of despair you usually get when England take the penalty shoot-out route to ruin. I suppose it's because the element of drama was taken away this time. It was more a depressed feeling, because you suddenly realised that we are years behind the Germans, not to mention a few other countries.

Other countries like Brazil. For all the talent at their disposal, Dunga, their coach, still finds the need to play with two holding players. So why not England? The fact that they had beaten Chile six times out of six, scoring 25 goals in the process, did not mean they could take liberties against their fellow South Americans in their second-round tie in Johannesburg. Nor did they. But there is enough about the five-time champions to know that when Howard Webb, the English referee, denied them a penalty for a trip by Pablo Contreras on Lucio – a decision that may come back to haunt him when FIFA make their decision on who should referee the final – they would get another opportunity. And sure enough they did, in fact they got two in the next ten minutes, and Juan, with a header, and Luis Fabiano, with a pass from Kaka, converted them both.

I'm not sure whether regular watchers at the City of Manchester Stadium are feeling a bit peeved about the form of the rejuvenated Robinho or excited about his return there this summer, following his loan spell with Santos. His first goal of the tournament here was as overdue as it was deserved.

Brazil's opponents in Port Elizabeth on Friday will be the Netherlands, who showed Italy how to deal with Slovakian upstarts. The Dutch remain more pragmatic than pretty, but are developing a nice habit of winning, this being their eighth in succession. They have waited for the return of Arjen Robben from injury, just as England waited for Gareth Barry, only the Bayern Munich player's return proved to be worth waiting for. The opposition manager described him as 'a genius' whereas the hard-to-please Dutch manager Bert van Marwijk said he was 'not the man he used to be'. Either way, he is a player worth having in one's side, as he showed in opening the scoring. He's a flying machine. The excellent Wesley Sneijder was the creator then and later the scorer of the second goal before the prolific Robert Vittek replied with a meaningless penalty in the last minute.

Tuesday 29 June

Paraguay 0 Japan 0 (aet; Paraguay win 5–3 on pens)
Spain 1 Portugal 0

The impossible job appeared to be taking its toll on its latest incumbent, as Capello spoke unconvincingly of the absent friends who might rescue England's standing among the super-powers of world football. But who was he talking about? Rio Ferdinand? David Beckham? Michael Owen? No. The kind of players he had in mind were Bobby Zamora and Owen Hargreaves. England's plight is indeed desperate.

The Football Association announced that they would give a decision on Capello's future after a fortnight's deliberation, having taken no time at all in removing the get-out clause in his contract less than four weeks ago. Suddenly Capello is no longer the manager who must be retained at all costs, although the feeling is he will stay. He threw up a variety of names who might now get a chance: Adam Johnson, Theo Walcott, Kieran Gibbs, Gabriel Agbonlahor and Jack Wilshere, as well as the brittle Hargreaves and the non-prolific Zamora, none of whom exactly set the pulse racing.

When the subject turned to winter breaks, it all began to sound depressingly familiar. The fact that fatigue doesn't seem to have affected the numerous other players at this World Cup who earn their living in the Premier League was conveniently overlooked. He defended his choice of 4–4–2 by saying: 'I think you can decide on different styles, but always the success of the style depends on the form of the players. We have played this style for a long time and results were good.'

He blamed individual error for three of Germany's four goals, for which he received support from a man whose World Cup also ended before it had begun, in 2002. Never afraid of criticising players, even when he was a player himself at Old Trafford, Roy Keane thought the players should take the Three Lions' share of responsibility. Now he is a fully paid-up member of the managers' union, he is even less likely to let slackers get away with it.

'To keep criticising and questioning the manager is crazy,' said the Ipswich Town boss. 'He didn't do anything wrong in the qualifying campaign and now, all of a sudden, he's not the top man any more. They should leave him to get on with the job. He is brilliant and England are lucky to have him. They [the players] have to take a long, hard look at themselves. They get away with murder. The goals they conceded against Germany, particularly the first couple, had nothing to do with Capello's choice of system or tactics. It wasn't a case of getting overrun in midfield. It was just very bad defending.'

The *Sun* newspaper left the players in no doubt who they thought was to blame, with a front page headline large enough for anyone walking past an airport news stand in the arrivals hall to read. Under the sub-heading 'Today's weather' it said: 'Sunny outlook in many areas but depression over Heathrow as shower drifts in from South Africa.'

Meanwhile, FIFA kept their silence on the refereeing blunders in the games affecting England and Mexico, which could have been avoided by giving technology a chance.

The second anniversary of Spain's crowning as European champions was a good time to assert their parochial authority in the battle of Iberia. Portugal were unbeaten in their previous twenty matches, but they remain in the words of their own manager Carlos Queiroz 'very pragmatic'. They lacked the cutting edge to trouble Spain and so resorted to the role of spoilers, although I have to say they do defend fantastically well. As a result, it took a long time for Spain to translate their superiority into goals, or rather a goal. But it was a goal worth waiting 64 minutes for. It was instigated by Andres Iniesta, and aided and abetted by an inspired little backheel from Xavi Hernandez. David Villa missed with his first opportunity, but made no mistake with the second.

Prior to that, Fernando Torres flattered to deceive, starting brightly only to fizzle out, eventually being substituted by the livelier Fernando Llorente. Portugal departed the competition in cynical fashion with a straight red card for Ricardo Costa for aiming an elbow at Joan Capdevila, while Cristiano Ronaldo showed his all-round contempt for everything and everyone by spitting at the camera as he left the field. Any sympathy one might have had for this one positive individual amid so much negativity rapidly dissolved.

Japan had been hoping to become the first Asian side to beat a South American nation, but that necessitated them putting the ball between the Paraguayan posts, which proved difficult for them in normal time, extra time and ultimately the penalty shoot-out, which they lost.

Netherlands 2 Brazil 1

Uruguay 1 Ghana 1 (aet; Uruguay win 4–2 on pens)

They had impressed us defensively, but what kind of compliment is that to a Brazilian team? We should have feared the worst when they struggled to score against North Korea. How ironic that they should be undone by the sort of individual flair that their coach Dunga had largely turned his back on. Arjen Robben, as if Brazilian-born, teased and tormented them to the point of distraction, whereupon even their new-found discipline deserted them. Expect a return to more familiar Brazilian ways four years from now.

And yet, for 45 minutes, they had appeared nicely on course for a sixth title, following Robinho's smooth tenth-minute goal. But Robben's constant probing eventually paid dividends when he earned a cheap free-kick after 53 minutes. He played it to Sneijder, who drove the ball head-high towards Julio Cesar's goal. It might have been comfortably cleared, but the ball skimmed off the head of Felipe Melo; the goal was originally credited as an own goal, and would have been the first conceded by Brazil in 97 World Cup ties, but was finally given by FIFA to the Dutchman. Sneijder's second goal, a quarter of an hour later, was definitely his as the little man got his head to a cross from Robben that had been helped on by Dirk Kuyt.

A fractious affair like this could have only one conclusion and, with 17 minutes left to play to save the match, Melo compounded his earlier error by being sent off for a vicious stamp. It was the sixth dismissal of his career for club and country. The team that they said was in Dunga's image had made an ignominious exit and his four-year reign as manager was over.

It was a cruel end to Africa's involvement in this World Cup at Soccer City, and the rights and wrongs of Luis Suarez's handball which denied Ghana a certain victory and Africa their first semi-finalist will be debated long and hard. All I would say is that the Uruguayan striker did what any player would instinctively do. That doesn't make it right, and although he suffered the penalty, when it came to penalties it was Ghana who suffered.

In a perfect world Asamoah Gyan would have converted the spot-kick – the last kick of the match – but he didn't. I thought it took enormous courage to then step up and take the first kick in the penalty shoot-out. I felt for them because in extra time they were the team who were trying to win it. Uruguay looked as though they were playing for the penalties, which they probably thought might be a bit too much for Ghana. And so it proved.

It also took some nerve for Sebastian Abreu to finish with a Panenka-style dink. I remember scoring one like that in a Rumbelows Cup semi-final for Tottenham against Nottingham Forest. The Forest keeper Mark Crossley had brilliantly saved my penalty in the 1991 FA Cup final. I knew he liked to dive early, so I chipped one down the middle and he ended up hitting his head against the post. The only thing is, when you miss with one of those, as I did against Brazil in attempting to equal Bobby Charlton's goal-scoring record, you don't half look an idiot.

Saturday 3 July

Argentina 0 Germany 4
Paraguay 0 Spain 1

Well at least we scored. In fact we scored two. On second thoughts, whichever way you look at it, it was a thumping for both England and Argentina. With hindsight, it was inevitable that Argentina's exciting if naive approach would be punished by a team like Germany. It is going to take a very special side to stop them. They were supposed to be a team in the making. On the evidence of this match they've already made it.

Germany really are a thrilling side to watch, far removed from the German stereotypes. They have youth, pace and a growing confidence in their own ability: a dangerous combination. Bastian Schweinsteiger may be only 25, but he has been capped 79 times for his country and he was at the heart of this German master-class. Maradona could only watch on helplessly as his team were cut to ribbons. No amount of hugs and kisses are going to make the hurt go away.

It was a great shame that Lionel Messi could not be given the right support to show what he can do. It was a bit like Maradona in the 1982 World Cup: the ability was there, but the supporting parts were found wanting. Ultimately, Maradona's simplistic tactics were horribly exposed. It took Gemany just three minutes to point up their deficiencies, as Thomas Müller headed home Schweinsteiger's free-kick. What a pity he will miss the match against Spain through suspension because of an innocuous handball. Miroslav Klose, in his hundredth international, scored twice in the second half to take his World Cup total haul to fourteen, just one behind the record of Brazil's Ronaldo. Arne Friedrich was Germany's other scorer.

Spain's progress to the repeat of the European Championship final of two years ago, when Fernando Torres scored the only goal, was far less impressive. Paraguay made life difficult for them and it wasn't until the 83rd minute that David Villa breached their defence. With Torres struggling to find his touch, Villa has been deployed in three different positions in this World Cup, but wherever he has played he has popped up with a goal.

He now has 43 in 63 matches for Spain. Villa is something

of an overnight success in ten years. That's how long it's taken the 28-year-old to secure a move to a major club, having recently joined Barcelona. Had he not missed a penalty against Honduras in the group stage, he would have been odds-on favourite to take the Golden Boot. That miss also prevented him from equalling Raul's record of 44 goals. The one he did get here came a little reluctantly, the ball striking one post before going in off the other.

Tuesday 6 July

Uruguay 2 Netherlands 3

So a European team will win the World Cup for the first time outside of Europe. That was the upshot of the Netherlands' narrow win against Uruguay, whose luck finally ran out – not before time Ghana may think.

I wasn't working, so I went to the game with my son George. It was a weird one: the first half was so poor and yet there were two wonder goals, especially the one from Giovanni van Bronckhorst, who was always a sweet striker of the ball when he was at Arsenal. It was probably the goal of the tournament, hit from all of forty yards, but moments before Mark van Bommel had committed the most horrendous foul and got away with it as he has on numerous occasions at this World Cup – that was Uruguay's first bit of bad luck.

Van Bommel's the kind of uncompromising midfielder you want in your side, but not against you. He's one of four top-class players they have, the others being Sneijder, Robben and Robin van Persie; otherwise the rest are journeymen. It's about bringing the best out of people, which England didn't do. It's amazing what a bit of togetherness, organisation and spirit can achieve.

Uruguay's second bit of bad luck came after Diego Forlan had pulled them level with another fine strike of the Jabulani ball he masters so well. A shot from Sneijder, which put the Dutch 2–1 ahead, should have been disallowed, we realised later, because van Persie was standing in an offside position as the shot deflected in off Maxi Pereira. It was Sneijder's fifth goal of the tournament, not bad for a midfielder. Moments later the South American participation in this World Cup was as good as over, as Robben headed home a cross from Dirk Kuyt. Pereira's 90th-minute reply proved to be an irrelevance.

I'm really looking forward to tomorrow's match, which I think is absolutely fifty-fifty. You would say Germany look stronger going into it, they're the form team, but it's really hard to come away with three great performances on the bounce. Spain have done what Germany usually do: which is get to the semi-finals without playing that well. You just think there is a performance in them somewhere.

Wednesday 7 July

Germany 0 Spain 1

As Joachim Löw, Germany's manager, said afterwards, 'Spain are the best team in the world,' and this was their best performance in this World Cup. It was a terrific game, it just lacked a few goals, as many of Spain's games have done. It's a pity their reputation has preceded them, because Germany, like everyone else, were frightened of what they could do and as a result were too defensive. So the two greatest football nations never to have won the World Cup will be contesting the final, which seems appropriate. I think Spain will have too much for the Netherlands, who will probably sit back against them like everyone else. Hopefully, Spain will score early, which will bring the Dutch out to play. Then we should have a match. This World Cup has become Europe's party. It's the seventh time out of the last eight that Europe have had at least three teams in the semi-finals. And best of all, we will have a brand-new champion.

Spain's passing, their patience, their movement, the way they find space – it's just a joy to behold. Germany, who were without the suspended Thomas Müller, may have regrets about the way they played, but if you can't get the ball . . . You're probably better off having a go against them. The only team to cause them problems so far have been Paraguay, who pressed them high up the pitch in the first half. The trouble is you can't do that for ninety minutes. Spain are not a great counter-attacking side, because their game is about short passes so they can't get to the other end of the field that quickly. Instead, they kill you bit by bit.

We said about England that if Wayne Rooney wasn't playing or in form, we didn't stand a chance. With Spain you could take any of their big players out of their line-up and they would still be a force to be reckoned with. Indeed, Fernando Torres, to all intents, hasn't been there for them because of his physical condition, but it hasn't damaged their overall effectiveness. You just look at their bench and weep: Torres, Cesc Fabregas, Pepe Reina, Carlos Marchena, David Silva – all great players, who would be a valuable addition to just about every other team at this World Cup.

Pedro Rodriguez, the Barcelona player, was one of those peripheral players who was given a chance here in place of Torres and he was quite superb, apart from failing to spot that Spain had a man over late on. He surely did enough to keep his place for the final. And how good was it to see that old Barca stalwart score with a stunning header? The way he plays, Carles Puyol could have been English – the best of English, I mean. He's a player who always keeps himself in excellent physical shape; the perfect role model.

Germany can be very proud of their young side and their young manager. His contract expired on 30 June, not even the end of the championship, and the German FA have extended it only so he can take charge of the team for the third-place match. No talk of contracts until the job has been done – FA please note. But Löw's not bothered: 'No matter who the coach is, this team is there to stay,' he said. 'We have a core, a nucleus, and their development has just started. It is far from over.'

Doesn't it make you just a little bit envious?

Saturday 10 July

Uruguay 2 Germany 3

I can't for the life of me understand why they play the third-place play-off; after you've lost a semi-final, all you want to do is go home. It's a game no one wants to play in – mind you, England might have taken it. Full credit then to Germany and Uruguay for putting on a decent competitive show with plenty of goals – although I was pleased for them they didn't have to stay for a further half-hour, as they might have done had Forlan's 92nd-minute free-kick gone in, instead of striking the bar.

As has been his wont, Thomas Müller put Germany ahead with his fifth goal of the tournament. He has made himself at home in that right-wing position; at Bayern Munich he's more central. Edinson Cavani soon equalised for Uruguay and, perhaps mindful of the fact that they have a parade through the streets of Montevideo to come on Monday, not to mention a date with President Jose Mujica, Forlan then put them ahead with a typically acrobatic volley. The Uruguayan keeper Fernando Muslera, who was at fault for the first goal, did not cover himself in glory at a cross from Jerome Boateng and Marcell Jansen was given an easy equaliser. Uruguay's record of not having beaten a European team since the 1970 World Cup was confirmed when Sami Khedira headed a late winner.

Netherlands 0 Spain 1 (aet)

Rinus Michels would have turned in his grave, but I'm certain the founding father of Total Football would have rejoiced in Spain's hour of triumph over thuggery. Who would have thought the Dutch could stoop so low? And the frightening thought is, it almost succeeded. What a dreadful message that would have sent to youngsters around the world who already copy enough the cynical practices of professional footballers – and what a shocking irony and dishonour to the names of great players like Cruyff, Neeskens and Rensenbrink, who pulled up just short in this competition.

Spain are a far, far better role model and thoroughly deserving winners of this World Cup for the first time in their history. They may not have scored as prolifically as the best of the boys from Brazil, but they are just as easy on the eye. Indeed, their eight goals were the fewest scored by any champion team. It was case of 'one-nil to the Spanish' from the knockout stages onwards, but that was only because their opponents were more intent on stopping them scoring than being creative themselves.

I would like to be able to say that the English made the final after all and gave an excellent account of themselves, but it has to be said that Howard Webb refereed a difficult game not very well. He brought the yellow card out of his pocket 14 times, which was more than enough for any game, but he didn't bring out the red one soon enough. A Dutchman – notably either

Mark van Bommel or Nigel de Jong, preferably both – could have been, should have been, sent off more than an hour before John Heitinga finally was in extra time. No one wants to see a player sent off in a final, but sometimes it has to be done – even in the first half.

Robben said beforehand he would 'prefer to win a very ugly game than to lose a beautiful game', but I cannot believe such a creative player as he can have meant something as grotesquely ugly as this. Spain were no angels, mind you – although they may play like one – but in the face of such provocation you would have to be a saint not to respond.

It was a bit rich that the Netherlands should complain about Webb's handling of the game: they should have looked at themselves first. What really seemed to upset them was his decision not to award the Dutch a free-kick and send off Carles Puyol for a second yellow card for a foul on Robben with six minutes of normal time remaining. For once, the former Chelsea player was honest enough to stay on his feet and he did so because he thought he might score, but the excellent Iker Casillas denied him as he had done on a previous occasion.

It's going to be interesting to see how much Vicente del Bosque's side is imitated. There probably isn't enough of an end product for some British tastes, but that's the only criticism you could level at them. But that's because their intricate short passing – known as *futbol sala* or *tic-tac* in Spain – means that too many bodies have to be used in the build-up play and they can't get enough of them in the final third. What I find so amazing is that they send on a substitute, and he immediately settles into their passing patterns without disruption. And every single one of them is comfortable on the ball; not for nothing is their centre-back Gerard Pique known as 'Piquenbauer'.

I was so pleased that my personal favourite, Andres Iniesta, should score the winning goal, courtesy of Cesc Fabregas's pass. It was a shot that needed to be well struck to beat Maarten Stekelenburg; suffice to say about him that Edwin van der Sar wasn't missed for a moment. Forlan was chosen as the winner of the Golden Ball for the player of the tournament, and certainly his ability to master the Jabulani at free-kicks deserved some sort of prize, but for me Iniesta was the best player in South Africa. I used to think there wasn't much to choose between him and Xavi, but I realise now that Iniesta is that little bit more special, a little bit more cute.

Just to mention what Fabio Capello quite rightly described as the 'terrible Jabulani' ball one final time, it was almost responsible for an absurd goal when Gregory van der Wiel played the ball back to Casillas, after Spain had deliberately put it out of play, and the ridiculous bounce of the ball took it over his head and very nearly into the net. I'd like to think had it gone in, the Dutch would have allowed Spain to equalise, as they gave possession from the resulting corner straight back to Spain.

It was a pity Villa could not score the goal he needed to claim the Golden Boot – although how he failed to in the 68th minute when Heitinga got back to make an amazing block I will never know. Instead, the prize went to Müller, who hadn't impressed me for Bayern Munich before this World Cup. He got five goals, like Villa, Forlan and Sneijder, but won on assists. His namesake

Gerd Müller got twice as many in 1970, while even yours truly managed six – which has been the norm – when he won it in 1990. The great Just Fontaine holds the record with a staggering thirteen in 1958.

Television people are as competitive as anyone, and we at the BBC were delighted with our viewing figures for the final. We peaked at 17.9 million to ITV's 3.8 million and averaged 15.1 to their 3.3. What it did show was that, even without England's participation and, furthermore, after some woeful performances by the national team, interest remained incredibly high. The actual viewing figures were probably at least double this amount because they don't take into consideration that large groups of people watch an event like this.

It has not been a memorable World Cup – the vuvuzelas can't be forgotten quickly enough. But hopefully Spain, the European and new world champions, will have left a legacy that will cause us to look back on these finals with greater fondness.

12

Capello: yesterday's man?

Somewhere between qualifying for the World Cup finals and the competition proper England, not for the first time in their history, lost all perspective when it came to expectations. Many of us had hoped that the team would come with a blindside run in these finals, as one of the less-fancied sides, and take the world by surprise. Fat chance. England, for some unearthly reason, suddenly became one of the favourites and the weight of expectation dragged them down, exposing them as an ageing side with serious deficiencies for which their illustrious manager Fabio Capello failed to compensate.

The fact that they were ultimately put out of their misery by their nemesis, Germany, of course only added to their misery and that of the nation. I cannot remember such a pitiful tournament performance from an England team, be it in World Cups or European Championships. It was a performance without heart, savvy and least of all desire. Fear consumed them from the start and held them in its grip like rabbits caught in a headlight until Germany rode roughshod over them – and our dreams – at the start of the knockout stages. It wasn't long ago that we viewed quarter-finals as an underachievement, despite the fact we have done better than this only once away from home and the fact that we have won just nine games in the knockout stages of major tournaments in our history: a rethink of our potential may be necessary.

It made Sven-Goran Eriksson's reign look like a golden era. The only English winner as far as I could see was Wayne Bridge, and while I'm sure he was relieved he chose not to take part in what turned out to be a fiasco, I'm also sure he was just as disappointed as the rest of us with England's lame effort. England teams have returned home from tournaments in the past, even reasonably successful ones, with the odd fall guy or two in their midst, but never a whole team of them. Almost to a man they underperformed. England started disappointingly against the United States . . . well, actually, that's not quite true: Steven Gerrard, their inspirational captain, got them off to a flyer with a goal after just four minutes. The euphoria didn't last, though. They then went from bad to worse, against Algeria, played averagely to eke out a 1–0 victory against that famous footballing nation of Slovenia and then capitulated against Germany.

The winter weather of South Africa was expected to be a

major factor in England's favour, unlike in previous World Cups when the finals have invariably been staged in warm climates. In the event, it counted for little because, with the exception of the game against Slovenia, we never really produced the high-tempo style of football for which English teams, if not always England, are famed.

If England were to be successful, and by that I mean at least reach the semi-finals, we all knew that Wayne Rooney, as the team's lucky jewel, would have to be at his talismanic best, which meant both scoring and creating goals. In the event, for whatever reason, he did neither and performed nowhere near the level he had maintained throughout the season for club and country until injured in late March. Far from being one of the stars of the tournament, he had little more than a walk-on part.

His Manchester United manager, Sir Alex Ferguson, blamed expectations rather than injury or end-of-season fatigue. 'I think there was such expectation on him,' he said. 'There was talk he was going to be the player of the tournament. Don't forget – that was the prelude to the whole thing – he was going to be the star, he was going to outshine them all – Messi, Ronaldo. And he's not got great experience of [playing in] the World Cup really. You wait, in four years' time you'll see a different player.'

Hopefully, we will. But we won't be seeing many of his teammates playing in this competition in four years' time. For many it was their last hurrah, so all the more reason for them to give it a go, you would have thought. David James, who will be 40 in August, may feel he did. But I'm sure the likes of 31-year-old Rio Ferdinand, who withdrew on the eve of the finals through injury, Frank Lampard (32) and Gerrard (30) will bitterly regret not being able to do better, not being able to show the world what they were capable of. I feel very sorry for them, because I know what a fabulous opportunity they have missed. If you are at all patriotic, nothing compares to national success at a World Cup; I doubt not even winning a Champions League final does. Apart from anything else, it can be the making of an individual, as one or two of the boys from '66 know only too well.

Even allowing for the ridiculous hype, England fell woefully short of the standards expected of them after what had been an excellent qualifying campaign. With hindsight, we probably read too much into that. Perhaps that was our first mistake. We knew at the outset it was a group from which it would be easy to qualify, even if it did pit us against our old rivals Croatia, but a team can only beat what is placed in front of them, and England did that efficiently enough.

Because we didn't face better opposition in the qualifiers, the team was not properly tested. Perhaps more importantly, neither were the tactics. Capello has played 4–4–2 most of his career, and with unbelievable success at some of the powerhouses of European club football, such as AC Milan, Juventus and Real Madrid. But what was successful ten years ago or even five years ago is not necessarily successful today and his tactics looked outdated in South Africa.

Whether that was mainly because Capello didn't have the players to pull off those tactics, or because they were no longer effective in today's game, it is hard to say because, when all is said and done, the game is about players rather than tactics. But there could be no doubt that England repeatedly found themselves outnumbered in midfield by the many teams who opted for a more fluid 4–5–1 formation or the more conservative 4–2–3–1 shape. Worse still, when England did find themselves overrun in midfield, he did nothing to remedy it, as you would imagine a coach of his capability would – indeed as a coach of much less capability would.

During the qualifiers he came to the conclusion that he got the best out of Rooney – as he needed to do – whenever the burly Emile Heskey was playing alongside him and taking the physical strain off the United striker. This encouraged him – I would suggest mistakenly – to persist with 4–4–2, when what he needed to do was take a long look at Rooney in the role in which he was so successful last season for United, which was playing on his own up front. Most of the time at Old Trafford, he had wide support from Ryan Giggs and Luis Antonio Valencia. Capello may not have had quite that kind of support in his England set-up, but he did have great central midfielders in Steven Gerrard and Frank Lampard, who could arguably offer Rooney as good if not better support than Giggs and Valencia.

Capello couldn't see it and plugged on with Heskey, occasionally giving games to the Tottenham strikers Jermain Defoe and Peter Crouch, who would score with some regularity and then be put back in their box. Had England suffered one or two heavy reverses during the qualifying campaign, he might have felt compelled to look at different tactics. It was notable that whenever England did come up against quality opposition, like Spain and Brazil, they lost, albeit not heavily but fairly conclusively all the same, or they struggled, as they did against the Netherlands. A second-half comeback from two goals down probably put a false complexion on that particular performance. And remember, these friendlies came at a time when confidence was high.

Because England, in the main, were winning their matches playing the way Capello knew best, he saw no reason to change. Heskey almost became a key player, which I found worrying. I have known him since he was a boy at my old club Leicester, and he is a thoroughly honest professional with certain attributes, such as a physical presence. But he has never been and never will be a goalscorer, even at club level, never mind international level. He is the sort of player who can be a handful for the less accomplished teams around the world, but not those who qualify for World Cup finals. To them he is mere fodder. However, to suggest that Heskey was one of the main culprits for our failure would be wrong.

Perhaps the biggest criticism of this England team was its lack of balance, which, unbelievably, Capello attempted to correct by playing Steven Gerrard wide on the left. The left side of England's midfield has been a problem for as long as I can remember, and it will never be properly solved until, guess what, you play a left-side player or at least someone disciplined enough to play that role, which Gerrard palpably is not. Anyone who has ever seen him play knows he is at his best in a central position, as he invariably is these days at Liverpool, and that he is something of a free spirit. To restrict him to a specific role, worse still one to which he is totally ill-suited wide on the left – the 'graveyard shift', as he refers to it – is to minimise the contributions of an exceptional player. On top of that, it just doesn't work. Some would go as far as to say that it is virtually impossible for England to play well against good opposition when they are set up in such a fashion with the players that they have.

If Capello didn't see the warning signs in the qualifiers, he must have seen them in the three friendly matches England played prior to the World Cup, which again, because they won (in the case of the match against Japan more through good fortune than anything else), meant they came up smelling of roses instead of fertiliser. The first half against Japan was nothing short of a jumbled mess. And then in the second half, Capello brought on Joe Cole and for a short while deployed him behind Rooney, who was then operating as a lone striker. The improvement was significant. Okay, it wasn't Gerrard in that role in the hole behind the striker – the 'sausage roll', as Cole calls it – but Cole could do the job just as well. Had the penny finally dropped with Capello, we wondered, because he was uncharacteristically effusive about the player afterwards.

'Joe Cole is an intelligent player,' he said. 'He can play in different positions. I know him and I'm very happy with him. He's in a good moment and he's fresh because he didn't play a lot of games [this season]. In the second half he played very, very well.'

In South Africa it was as though Cole's contribution that day never happened. We didn't see him again until the third game of the group matches and then only as a late substitute.

Apart from reasons of imbalance, Capello needed to change the tactics to offset the team's most glaring deficiency in defence:

pace. Ferdinand, our one and only central defender with real pace, had been struggling with his form and fitness even before the season began, but even an 80 per cent fit Ferdinand was better than no Ferdinand at all, we thought. It wasn't long before we got no Ferdinand at all. In a training session shortly after the team's arrival in South Africa, he damaged his knee ligaments when Heskey fell on him. His World Cup was over and to all intents so was England's, and one suspects, judging by the grave tone in which he delivered the news to a press conference, Capello knew it.

Replacing Ferdinand the captain was the easy part; replacing Ferdinand the central defender rather more difficult. England's World Cup had begun to smack of desperation even before then with the call-up of Jamie Carragher after a three-year international hiatus. Unlike Paul Scholes, who declined a last-minute invitation to return to the international fold after a six-year absence, Carragher agreed. The opportunity to work with such a renowned coach, one sensed, would be more for his benefit than England's. What Capello needed at the heart of his defence was youth and pace, not still more experience. At least the 32-year-old was fit, which was something.

Having promised that he would not take any player to the World Cup who was not completely physically sound, Capello went and took a whole treatment room full of sick players and would have taken even more if he could. He was deterred from taking the United midfielder Owen Hargreaves by Sir Alex, who must have pointed out to him that a 92nd-minute appearance as a substitute in United's penultimate game of the season after

20 months' inactivity did not constitute the ideal preparation for a World Cup. As it turned out, he was spot on because, as the World Cup drew to a conclusion, Ferguson announced that Hargreaves would miss the start of the new season after returning to the United States to see a specialist about his knee problem. At least Ledley King plays matches, even if because of a debilitating knee injury he doesn't train, so his place in the squad was a given, while Gareth Barry was allowed as long as possible to prove his fitness – if not his match fitness – after an ankle injury.

But the real fun and games didn't start until England arrived in South Africa. It had been apparent throughout the season that Capello was undecided as to who his No. 1 goalkeeper should be, but one hoped he would settle on someone before the squad arrived in South Africa. Not only did he not make his mind up, but he left it until two hours before the opening match kicked off before telling the three keepers which one of them was playing. I can't believe that contributed to Robert Green's dreadful gaffe, which gifted the United States an equaliser and ultimately cost England dearly, but it must have added to the uncertainty that was beginning to pervade the squad.

Capello had been hoping that between two half-fit central defenders, in King and Ferdinand, he might get one whole tournament. Instead he got next to nothing. With Ferdinand ruled out, King assumed the responsibility for playing the role of Ricardo Carvalho to John Terry. Knees may be the big issue with King, but within minutes of Gerrard's early goal King was telling Terry that his groin was hurting. He was eventually substituted at half time and his World Cup was over, too. At least he could claim that as long as he was playing England were unbeaten.

It's hard to believe that England, the team that not so long ago was described as the Golden Generation, could play any worse than this and yet six days later they did. The performance against Algeria plumbed new depths, and one of the most seriously afflicted was Rooney, whose ball control completely let him down at times. Some critics even advocated that he be dropped, which just weeks earlier would have been unthinkable. If, with David James restored between the posts, they never looked like conceding, they also never looked like scoring and a goalless draw left them facing the distinct possibility that they could fail to qualify from one of the easiest groups in the competition. The situation caused for a drastic rethink of England's tactics, but Capello's head remained firmly embedded in the sand.

Tales of player unrest are always rife at moments like this in a tournament, and England's camp was no exception. The former captain, John Terry, seemed to exceed his authority when, on behalf of the players – or so he thought – he informed the press that the players were calling for a clear-the-air meeting with Capello, which did not go down well with the manager, nor did his thinly veiled suggestion that his Chelsea team-mate Joe Cole should be in the side. Some thought Terry still bore a grudge against Capello for relieving him of the England captaincy over the Bridge affair, but the Chelsea captain is a natural leader and was probably doing what came naturally to him. As much as the media would have us believe otherwise, this was not a mutinous camp, unlike that of the French.

Capello is nothing if not his own boss, and after all the sabre-rattling, all he did in the way of changes was to replace Heskey with Defoe for the crucial upcoming match with Slovenia, which, I suppose, was some kind of improvement. At least now England had half a chance of scoring a goal and a half-chance is all Defoe needs – in the event, exactly what he accepted. It came courtesy of a teasing right-wing cross from James Milner, the kind he was all too capable of delivering. He hadn't done that against the United States, when perhaps he was still recovering from a stomach virus, but he managed it on a few occasions in that first half against Slovenia. After that this crucial front-line service mysteriously vanished, never to be seen again. Gerrard is not the kind to supply that type of cross and, in this tournament, Ashley Cole seldom got far enough forward to do so. Consequently, our strikers were starved.

The pressure was obviously getting to Capello, judging by the demonstrative manner in which he celebrated the Slovenia victory afterwards with his players, shaking the hand of his former captain Terry and bear-hugging Gerrard, his new captain. Nine months earlier, when his players were celebrating qualification, it was noticeable that he kept his distance from them like a latter-day Alf Ramsey. Such behaviour didn't become him, but now was no time to remain aloof and distant, not if he wanted to keep his players on side.

Again, it was a case of the opposition not being good enough to seriously test our defence, but very soon someone would be and then there would be no coming back from it, no second chance to reconsider our methods. It was painfully obvious to everyone except Capello that we needed two holding players to protect the back four. If those tactics were good enough for the likes of Brazil and the Netherlands, to name but two, they were certainly good enough for England. Instead, all we got was a half-fit, one-paced Barry, who, anyway, isn't a defensive mid-fielder, well though he had performed in that role in the past. Michael Carrick could have provided that extra security, but was never given an opportunity, and Scott Parker, one of the seven omitted from the final squad, would have at least been dogged.

If you have a defensive weakness in your team, then you organise it in such a way that makes you less easy to beat. It's common sense. Almost every team at this World Cup did that, except for England – and there were quite a few teams whose individual parts were no better than ours. It doesn't mean you have to turn yourself into the world's most negative team, as Greece did in 2004, but you have to be pragmatic about these things. With proper organisation this team could still have come good, but they were handicapped by their manager's tactics and as a result the players lost confidence in themselves and proba-bly him, too. The win against Slovenia just sustained the charade.

One would have thought it was finally time to stop playing games when the United States' late winner against Algeria meant that, as runners-up in Group C, we would face Germany instead of Ghana in the round of 16. But instead we just kept bumbling along in the same incoherent manner, which meant that we went into the game in Bloemfontein, like all the rest, on a left wing and a prayer. Germany, in the words of England's long-time torturer Franz Beckenbauer, 'took us apart'.

When the world champions Italy went out of the competition in the group stages, their manager Marcello Lippi fell on his sword, saying: 'I evidently was not able to prepare them as I had hoped. If a team plays as poorly as we did for seventy-five minutes [against Slovakia], there can be only one culprit: the manager. I thought we were ready – clearly we were not.' Unlike his fellow Italian, Capello still has a couple of years to run on his contract and as such is entitled to see it through. Furthermore, he wants to. I can't for the life of me understand why anyone would want to give a manager a four-year contract, never mind pay them £4.8 million a year, but there it is.

The Football Association originally told Capello that they would need a fortnight to decide whether or not he was still the right man for them, having just a month earlier decided he most definitely was when they removed a get-out clause in his contract in order to deter would-be suitors like Inter Milan. Reports of in-depth inquiries into what went wrong in South Africa would take at least that long to digest, but as it happened, the FA decided after five days that Capello was still the right man for them. How much they were influenced by the fact that it would cost them £12 million to pay off him and his backroom staff we may never know. Removing get-out clauses can prove an expensive business.

His performance in the immediate aftermath did not bode well and smacked of knee-jerk reactions instead of considered responses to our problems, like his suggestion that he should have scrapped the pre-tournament training camp in Austria and given them all a holiday. Can you imagine what would have happened had they underperformed after that? He would have been slaughtered. While it is obvious that new talent will need to be brought in, if only because older talent has reached the end of its life, it was probably unwise to be specific. Mentioning names such as Bobby Zamora, with all due respect to that player, is not likely to excite the public, never mind make them believe that next time things will be different.

Unlike when Eriksson became England's first foreign manager in 2001 in succession to Kevin Keegan, there are now born-and-bred English managers with decent credentials who could do the job, but the timing for one or two of them probably isn't right just now. Anyway, it's redundant talk because we have Capello for at least two more years. It's important, though, that he takes a long hard look at his performance in what was his first tournament as a national team manager. One would hope that he has learned some valuable lessons, because if he hasn't we could be in further serious trouble.

13

Looking on the bright side

While Germany's defeat to Spain may have proved Alan Hansen's dodgy maxim that you'll never win anything with kids, it did remind us that without proper youth development we might as well not bother to participate in World Cups. Germany's performance in South Africa should be an inspiration to us all – particularly England. It was after the humiliation of a defeat to England at Euro 2000 that the German FA demanded a complete revamp of its academy system and ten years on they are reaping the benefits.

Of course, the problem with English football is that you don't know who is running the show – the Football Association, Club England or the Premier League. In fact, you don't even know who is running the FA, who in the last couple of years has lost its commercial director, chief executive and independent chairman. But, whoever they are, until they are all singing from the same song sheet I can't see things improving greatly.

And yet there are reasons to be cheerful. Three days after England's ignominious exit from this World Cup, another England team won the UEFA European Under-17 Championship in Liechtenstein by beating Spain 2–1, which was good news for those who believe in omens. While it will be interesting to see how many players from those two sides eventually make the grade, at that age it's more about developing skills and good habits than winning football matches. It took us a long time to grasp that fact.

Gone, thank goodness, are the days when we would stick the biggest boys we could find in our team and muscle our way to victory against smaller, more skilful players: England schoolboy matches always used to look like catch-weight contests – except in terms of skill. At the sharp end, it's never been a game for giants, and this World Cup has only confirmed that fact with the most creative performances coming from the likes of Lionel Messi, David Villa, Wesley Sneijder, Carlos Tevez, Robinho and Diego Forlan – not a six-footer among them. In fact, earlier in his career, Villa got rejected by Oviedo because he was too small, so it's nice to know we're not the only ones who have got that wrong in the past.

There are some very good academies in England – Chelsea's, for example, is excellent. In fact the Germans, ironically, used one or two of ours as their template, but there are not enough of them and not enough money is spent on them. The Bundesliga clubs spend £80 million a year on their youth system, while their more affluent English counterparts spend just £30 million. Why? Because clubs, be they English or German, prefer to spend their money on the here and now. The German clubs were prevented from continuing such short-sighted practice because of their FA's omnipotence; they were told that if they didn't set up academies their licences wouldn't be renewed.

Sir Trevor Brooking, the FA's director of football development, has been deeply frustrated at his inability to push through change. But following the debacle in South Africa, hopefully there will now be a greater incentive to get something done, and he is hoping that his Future Game document, which is to be distributed among the academies, will revolutionise the way football is coached in England. 'I am acutely aware there are no quick fixes and easy answers, that we must focus on the long-term future of our game,' he said following England's exit, although he has been saying the same thing for ages. 'The key is that we must have more and better skilled coaches with more access to kids at an earlier age.'

England is lagging far behind the rest of Europe in that respect. Of those countries with coaches holding UEFA's A, B and Pro badges, Spain has 23,995, Italy 29,420 and Germany 34,970. And England? We have 2679. Enough said.

The Netherlands has a population one-third the size of England's, and a much inferior league, and yet they produce no end of talent, and have done so for thirty or forty years. English football may be multi-national these days, but the foreigners in it are playing an English style of pace and power and no little skill, which remains one of our attributes and why coach-loads of Dutch and other nationalities come to watch it every week. Not that we saw much pace and power during this World Cup.

It's at times like this when you wish English football had a commissioner. Brooking would get my vote. He's a football man through and through who understands the game and genuinely cares about it. He also understands the politics. I'm not sure there are many you could say that of in positions of power in our game today; it seems to me they are more interested in massaging their egos. Since England's surrender against Germany, I have heard any number of them giving their opinions on the ability of Fabio Capello as a manager, but what do they know about the game, other than putting their names in lights? What do they know about technique or tactics? As far as I am concerned, they have no more knowledge – and probably a lot less – than the average fan.

Brooking has advocated that Capello become more involved in player development, and while it would be good to have his input on that, international managers cannot afford to take a long-term view. In an ideal world, Capello would now start planning for the 2014 World Cup in Brazil, if not 2018, hopefully in England, and forget about the 2012 European Championship. But try selling that to the public, who want instant success just as much as the manager's paymasters. It's the same with clubs: there's not much point in a five-year plan if you are relegated that season. And yet those clubs who have been patient invariably reap the benefit: Manchester United, Arsenal, West Ham, Ipswich in the early 1980s.

With the right tactics, England can acquit themselves credibly at Euro 2012, no more than that. But I really do believe that the good work the academies are starting to do could begin to kick-in in about five years' time. At the 2014 World Cup, the South Americans should really come into their own. This World Cup started out brilliantly for them, but it was the Europeans who dominated in the end. Brazil will be different. Unfortunately, Capello can afford to look no further than England's next match, a friendly against Hungary at Wembley in August, which he *must* win. Never did a friendly take on so much importance.

His first job is to turn public opinion around. It's not going to be easy to regain the faith of the public or his players. His reputation has been badly stained by this World Cup, and he needs to put that right, if only for selfish reasons. He will want to show that he can be successful as a national team manager, just as he was as a club manager, even if, at 64, this may be his last mission in football. The job criteria haven't changed: pick the right team, the right tactics and win matches. He had trouble meeting each of those requirements in South Africa, notably the second. I believe in order to be successful he will have to change, unless he stumbles upon the right individuals to make 4–4–2 work. He is going to have to look at what the rest of the world is doing and take it on board. In short, he must stop being so stubborn.

There was no one he left at home, other than those who were ruled out by injury, who would have made a significant difference to the outcome in South Africa. Yes, some would have done marginally better than those who were selected, but other than perhaps getting a better balance in his squad, there was not a lot more that could have been done in terms of who he chose. So it comes back to tactics and man-management skills. Much has been written about what an unhappy camp it was, but in my experience camps are always unhappy when you are losing. It's funny how there were no stories of unrest coming out for a few days after the win against Slovenia.

Communication may have been an issue with Capello. He hasn't helped himself when it comes to the language. He almost hides behind this very poor English, and I do wonder how well he is able to convey his ideas and feelings to the players. Sven-Goran Eriksson's English may not have been very exciting, but at least he was able to get across his message. Capello has been in the job two and a half years now, and he really ought to be speaking the language more fluently than he is.

I realise it's a lot more difficult when you are older, but when I joined Barcelona in 1986, I had Spanish lessons three times a week for two years. Now you could argue that, having an English manager – Terry Venables – for the most part of my three-year stay, it wasn't really necessary, but I found it helped me enormously with my on-field and off-field relationships with team-mates and just made the whole experience more enjoyable. After three months there I got by with my Spanish, after six months I was reasonably good; after a year was I fluent and after two years I was actually thinking in Spanish.

Hopefully, Capello will have learned something about

running training camps at championships, which of course are rather different from those in pre-season when there is no pressure and everything is more relaxed. This, remember, was his first major championship as a national coach. I don't accept that the players were suffering end-of-season fatigue. In fact, the season just ended was less demanding than in previous years, because all of the leading English clubs were knocked out of the Champions League before the semi-final stage, and only Chelsea and Tottenham were involved late into the season in the FA Cup. Besides, there were enough players from the Premier League who were playing in this World Cup for other countries who didn't look worn out.

There is no doubt, though, that English players go into major championships often with slightly less of an edge than their rivals after a typically brutal English season. English-based players more than anyone need a mid-season break. Now there are only two ways that can be achieved and some will find both ways unpalatable. Either they reduce the Premier League to eighteen clubs – and none of the clubs is going to vote for that – or they get rid of one of the cup competitions. Many would say some of the leading clubs have already done that to all intents. The stock reply to all this is that clubs will just fly off somewhere to play lucrative friendlies instead.

England's problem looked more a psychological one to me. It's almost as though they froze, and yet we are talking about players who play in the Champions League and high-pressure Premier League matches before massive crowds. Handling pressure is part of top-class sport, but they definitely didn't look right in that respect, so Capello has to look at his preparations. And, of course, however professional they may want to be, it doesn't help if players know they are playing in a style or system that patently doesn't suit them.

It was said there were divisions in the camp, but you often get a bit of that and it doesn't usually affect the way a team plays. After all, Andy Cole and Teddy Sheringham never spoke to each other, but it didn't stop them forming a tremendous strike partnership and Manchester United winning the Treble.

Some people said that the England team didn't care enough, and that playing for their clubs was more important than playing for their country. Well, all I would say to that is nothing matters more to the people of Barcelona than Barcelona; nothing matters more to the people of Madrid than Real Madrid or Atletico Madrid, but it doesn't stop Spain from being the finest team in the world. Of course, the players care. It's a nonsense to suggest otherwise. I may be retired some sixteen years, but I don't believe the ambitions of professional footballers have changed that much. They still desperately want to do well for their country.

Footballers are a cross-section of working-class society, young men earning a lot of money at a young age. Within that you'll get your sensible ones and your not so sensible ones, as in other walks of life. Some will mistakenly flaunt their wealth, others won't. There may be a bit of yob culture in our country, but I don't believe they're that different to young footballers earning lots of money in other countries. And playing poorly at this World Cup, I can assure you, will hurt them. They have their professional pride after all.

Wayne Rooney has been singled out for criticism over and above poor form. There have even been complaints about his body language. But you have to remember that he must have been bitterly disappointed and incredibly frustrated with his own miserable performances, which bordered on the inept. When you are used to playing like an angel, that's bound to make you bloody grumpy. It would me.

It didn't look like Capello had the support of his players. Not like Maradona, anyway. I realise he is an extreme example, but ex-greats command an awful lot of respect. But you just know we would never take that risk – as Argentina did, as the Netherlands did with Frank Rijkaard and Marco Van Basten, as Germany did with Franz Beckenbauer and Jürgen Klinsmann. International management is different to club management. At international level, a manager doesn't have the time to work with players and build a relationship and understanding, so he has to make an immediate impact upon them. Maybe in the future we should have a look at someone like Alan Shearer, with an older head like Venables assisting him.

Five of the German team that humiliated England in Bloemfontein did almost exactly the same to another England team a year previously in Malmö, Sweden, in the final of the UEFA European Under-21 Championship, when they beat us 4–0 – you would have thought Stuart Pearce had suffered enough at German hands. At least we reached a final then. England's only graduate from that side was James Milner. One knee-jerk reaction to England's World Cup failure has been to suggest that we should have promoted more of our youngsters from that side, but there is no point in doing that unless they are up to the task, otherwise you will just destroy them. Germany's were clearly ready, ours, apart from Milner, weren't, though some thought that Theo Walcott and Adam Johnson might have been part of the squad.

There will be changes to Capello's squad, because major championships are always a watershed in that respect. It will happen over the course of the next year or two. It always does. Within a couple of years of Italia '90, Peter Shilton, Terry Butcher, Bryan Robson, Chris Waddle, Peter Beardsley and myself had all gone. Steven Gerrard, the captain, has said he wants to continue playing for England, and I'm certain he will do that at least until the European Championship, as will probably Frank Lampard and John Terry. I doubt if we will see David James between the posts again, and Rio Ferdinand may have to be even more judicious about when he plays, unless he makes a complete recovery from his various ailments. Likewise, Ledley King.

Capello's priority is to find more central defenders, preferably ones who are quick and comfortable on the ball; not qualities that are readily available anywhere, never mind just England. I'm sure the goalkeeping issue will resolve itself and that Capello will give an opportunity to Joe Hart, whom he likes. He was very close to using him in South Africa. In midfield, Capello must hope that Theo Walcott and Aaron Lennon come of age and add guile to their undoubted pace. He also needs to find a naturally defensive midfield player, hopefully somebody even better than Owen Hargreaves. In fact, ideally, he needs to find two of them.

As for attack, that's simple: play Wayne Rooney in the position he knows and likes best and the goals will follow.

Other countries will think we expect too much, and I'm sure most of the now grey-haired men who have managed England would agree. But the country who gave the game to the world, I believe, is still a major player and we should do so much better than we have done. It's unbelievable that we have failed to reach the final of a major competition in 44 years while 14 other European nations have done so. We have the desire, we have the ability and we have the financial wherewithal to do so. All we need is a bit more patience and the right method.